GW00385356

Hands Off
The Titanic!
(and The Californian)

by Monica Harding O'Hara

Dedicated to the Memory of
Captain Stanley Lord
A Man Maligned

First published 1989 by Countyvise Limited, 1 & 3 Grove Road, Rock Ferry, Birkenhead, Wirral, Merseyside L42 3XS.

Copyright © Monica Harding O'Hara, 1989.
Photoset and printed by Birkenhead Press Limited, 1 & 3 Grove Road, Rock Ferry, Birkenhead, Merseyside L42 3XS.

ISBN 0 907768 28 8.

Contents

Illustrations

Foreword
by Derek Whale

Of all sea dramas, none has captured the imagination like the sinking of the Titanic.

For the 77 years since she dived to her grave and settled in two parts on the bed of the North Atlantic, with the loss of 1,503 lives, she has become the greatest legend of the sea.

And now that she has been found, this four-funnelled former pride of the White Star Line, displacing 66,000 tons, has aroused worldwide interest once more.

There have probably been more stories written and told about the Titanic than about any other ship. Most of these have involved the same facts and theories, which have been constantly recycled ever since the liner hit an iceberg on her maiden voyage from Southampton to New York and foundered on the night of April 14/15, 1912.

But now, here is a book with a refreshing new angle on this long drawn-out drama . . .

Monica O'Hara, a graphologist of considerable expertise and success, has tackled the Titanic story from a most unusual viewpoint — by analysing the handwriting of numerous people closely associated with the ship.

She has revealed some fascinating aspects about them, and also explains how handwriting can 'fingerprint' character and behaviour.

For 50 years after the sinking, Captain Stanley Lord was maligned.

As master of the s.s.Californian, in the area of the Titanic at the time she was sinking, he was censured by a court of inquiry of failing to render assistance. He always emphatically denied this and died, a tragic figure, in 1962. Captain Lord, 'a first rate officer', was not guilty, says Monica O'Hara.

Bruce Ismay, chairman of the White Star Line, who remained a virtual recluse after the disaster, was pilloried until his death in 1937. He had taken a seat in a lifeboat.

Ismay's handwriting reveals 'a man with a mass of complexes'.

While wisely skirting the well-aired details of the disaster, Monica O'Hara has added a fascinating new dimension to the massive dossier on this famous ship, which made such an historical impact despite her very brief life.

Derek Whale is author of the following publications: SEE YOU ON THE ICE (a history of Liverpool Ice Rink), Pennant Studios, Liverpool: THE LOST VILLAGES OF LIVERPOOL (three volumes), Stephenson, Prescot and THE LINERS OF LIVERPOOL (three volumes), Countyvise, Rock Ferry.

Derek refers to me as Monica O'Hara, because that is the name I use in journalism, which profession we share. I reserve the Harding prefix for graphology.

HANDS OFF THE TITANIC

PROLOGUE:

The 'scapegoats'

Prologue

The Titanic should never have sunk. We all know that. We know, too, that many factors contributed to bring about the events of that fateful April night in 1912 when a spur of ice, projecting a few feet below the waterline, delivered an intermittent gash over a length of 300 feet of the greatest ocean liner ever built. And, as the water poured in, her life's blood poured out. The innocent-looking iceberg had delivered a death wound to the beautiful vessel and many of those who sailed in her.

It should never have happened, but it did, and it is only human to want to hold someone responsible. The finger of blame has always pointed at Captain Stanley Lord, master of the s.s. Californian who, according to legend, turned his back on the cries for help and allowed 1500 souls to perish.

Yet Captain Lord swore his vessel was nowhere near the beleagured ship at the time and, half a century after the tragedy, at the age of 84, he died — still protesting his innocence.

The accusations levelled at Bruce Ismay, the other 'scapegoat' were even more bizarre. Mr. Ismay was president of the White Star Line, who owned the ill-fated liner, and was one of the first class passengers aboard. He was accused of transvestism! His critics claimed he put on a frock and a fancy hat in order to leap from the deck into one of the lifeboats, thus surviving when hundreds of women and children perished.

What an intriguing and fascinating story is that of the Titanic. Would we ever discover what really happened? Was Captain Lord the heartless murderer he was made out to be?

Was Bruce Ismay the supreme coward everyone believed? Like so many others, I am passionately interested in the facts and fiction surrounding the great ship: and find it increasingly difficult to separate the two.

Or I did, until I stumbled across something which gave a clue to resolving the age-old mystery . . . which is what this book is all about, and which will be explained presently.

It is easy to be caught up in the propaganda machine which scarred and continues to scar the reputations of Lord and Ismay.

'The evil that men do lives after them, the good is oft interred within their bones . . .'

Shakespeare's words applied to Caesar, who was slain in 44BC. They could equally have applied to Lord and Ismay, whose characters were assassinated nineteen centuries later . . . .

Come forward in time . . . come now, to the present day. Allow me to introduce you to a man who knows more about one particular aspect of the Titanic than anyone else I have encountered. Meet Leslie Harrison. Due to his privileged position as the only professionally qualified person with whom Captain Lord discussed the matter at length (and to whom he entrusted all his papers), Mr. Harrison knows more about the Californian incident than any other living soul. The former General Secretary of the Mercantile Marine Service Association, who lives in retirement in Heswall, has spent much of his time writing about Captain Lord in an attempt to clear his name.

Mr. Harrison's home is just a few miles from Thurstaston, where the Ismay family resided at Dawpool Hall (now demolished); and a few miles, too, from the towns of Wallasey, where Captain Lord made his home, and Birkenhead, from where many of Titanic's crew originated.

It was in my role of journalist and book reviewer that I met Mr. Harrison; having arranged to interview him after receiving a copy of his latest book.*[1]

Our talk proved incredibly productive. Mr. Harrison showed me a collection of old documents relating to Titanic's movements on the night in question.

It was not the contents that captured my imagination, though they were fascinating enough in themselves. It was the handwriting on those documents that caught my eye, and the reason why they were so significant is because I am a graphologist. In other words, I analyse people's characters from their handwriting.

Never, in my wildest dreams, did I imgine I would be able to see — and touch — contemporary reports and notes relating to that eventful April night so long ago. They were not those of the Titanic, of course, which are probably still at the bottom of the ocean: though I have since been given access to a few notes and papers which were actually written on board a few hours before she disappeared forever and these will be analysed elsewhere in this book. The documents I had been allowed to examine at the outset were those from the Californian and from the inquiry investigating the movements of that ship on the night in question. They had been written by Captain Lord and several members of his crew.

I studied them briefly at the time; then in more depth later. And frankly, what I found was not at all what I had expected. It became abundantly clear why Captain Lord persistently protested his innocence and why, for that matter, Leslie Harrison did the same on his behalf.

The man **WAS** innocent.

The character assassination was totally unjustified. If ever a posthumous apology was called for, it was surely here, as we shall see . . . .

I am indebted to Mr. Harrison for giving me access to these very valuable writings. My gratitude is also extended to Chris Oakley, and Colin Hunt, editor and librarian, respectively of the Liverpool Echo, for allowing me to rummage extensively through the paper's yellowing records.

To Mr. Stanley Lord, son of the late Captain, I owe a special debt of gratitude. To me, as an analyst, it is inconceivable that Captain Lord was anything but a good and honourable man, despite what history and legend would have us believe.

John P. Eaton, author and historian for the Titanic Historical Society, has been a gem.*[2] His letters and their contents are always devoured instantaneously. I would like him to know how much I appreciate his contribution.

My thanks are also extended to Michael McCaughan*[3] at the Ulster Folk and Transport Museum, his friends at the Northern Ireland Tourist Board. And still in Belfast, I must thank the proprietors of Harland and Wolff for the signatures of their company's founders.

In Dublin, my main contact has been Fr. John Guiney, S.J., at Loyola House, Eglinton Road, who very kindly located those beautiful words penned by Fr. Francis Browne in memory of his erstwhile fellow passengers on Titanic. Fr. Browne's handwritten poem is reproduced in the Epilogue (where else?).

In Cork, my thanks go to fellow Titanic writer Tom Williams, his wife Mary and their family.

Back on home territory, my deepest gratitude is extended to Mike Stammers, director of Merseyside Maritime Museum and Howard Mortimer, music librarian at Birkenhead (music? . . . well, he is a walking encyclopaedia on Titanic, too!). Others who have helped in this rather offbeat area of research include J. Gordon Read, county archivist, Merseyside County Council County Archives Service, John Pile at Liverpool Chamber of Commerce; Harry Milsom, editor of Sea Breezes, Mrs. Pat Andrews of Wirral and Patrick Stenson, journalist, author*[4] and broadcaster.

Mrs. Andrews' grandfather, William Faulkner, was a first class steward on Titanic (and survived), but the outcome was not so happy for the great grand-uncle of Lucy Feeney, of Colwyn Bay. C. J. (Jack) Hurst, a stoker, was lost.

Thank you to Derek Whale, my colleague, fellow author and former shipping correspondent, for writing my foreword, and for translating maritime terminology into everyday language; to

Richard Garrett, former editor of The Cammell Laird Magazine, and currently a best-selling author*[5]; to 'the man with the hammer', Patrick Bogue, director of Onslow Auctions Ltd., (who conducted the Titanic auction at the Park Lane Hotel Ballroom in London on the 75th anniversary of the sinking).

A special word of acknowledgement is due to Dr. Brian Roy Stead who dug so deeply into his family tree to try and establish any possible relationship with the late, great William T. Stead, author, Spiritualist and social reformer who was lost in the tragedy. Despite all his digging, the doctor could not find anything tangible, but I'd like to thank him for his trouble, just the same.

Thank you, too, to Meredith Etherington-Smith, Deputy and Features Editor of Harpers and Queen for her help re Lady Lucy Duff-Gordon.

Southampton City Museum, the authorities at Cobh, the various relatives and descendents have all been remarkably helpful. So have innumerable publishers, editors and cognoscenti, in allowing me to quote them at sundry points throughout this book.

I'd like Esther, my daughter, to know how much I appreciate her efforts too . . . particularly in Sweden.

Most of all, I think I should say congratulations to the brave souls who corresponded with me in their own fair hands.

The title 'Hands Off the Titanic' has a double meaning: apart from the obvious reference to the handwriting samples, it is my own personal plea for the vessel never to be raised from the seabed. I feel strongly on that issue.

I must apologise for the reproduction of some of the samples which follow: notably on pages 34, 74, 80, 105 and 126. Age — and in some cases the North Atlantic — have taken their toll!

*[1] A Titanic Myth, The Californian Incident, by Leslie Harrison, Wm. Kimber, 1987.
*[2] Titanic, Triumph and Tragedy (A chronicle in Words and Pictures) and Titanic, Destination Disaster (The Legends and The Reality), both by John P. Eaton and Charles A. Haas; PSL, 1986 and 1987, respectively.
*[3] Titanic, by Michael McCaughan, Ulster Folk and Transport Museum, 1982.
*[4] Lights (The Odyssey of C.H. Lightoller), by Patrick Stenson, The Bodley Head, 1984.
*[5] Atlantic Disaster, by Richard Garrett, Buchan and Enright, 1987.

HANDS OFF THE TITANIC

CHAPTER ONE:
'Eejay'

Chapter One: 'EEJAY'

The Royal Mail Steamer, Titanic, was registered in Liverpool (though she never actually visited the port). She was built in Belfast, steamed on her trials to the Isle of Man and sailed from Southampton on her ill-fated maiden voyage.

Passengers were dropped off and collected first from Cherbourg, in France, then Queenstown (since renamed Cobh) in Ireland. After that, it should have been a straight run to New York; instead of which . . . well, the rest is history.

An analysis of Captain Smith's signature follows; those of Captain Lord and Benjamin Kirk will be examined in later chapters.*[6]

Figure 1

Captain Edward John Smith, went down with the Titanic. The signature illustrated above was written some years before the disaster; and this version of it is almost certainly a rubber stamp of the original, as used by the majority of shipmasters.

Allowing for the fact that, ideally, a sample of text should accompany the signature (to see if they concur) and that we are working on a copy of a copy, the conclusions to be drawn must, of necessity, be limited.

It can, however, be shown that Captain Smith had a sharp mind, a love of luxury and of music, a sense of self-importance and he was fond of company. He also manifests himself to have been more interested in physical than intellectual, or spiritual, pursuits. In other words, at the time of penning this particular signature, he would seem to have been quite active, sexually . . . a real ladies' man.

How can such conclusions be drawn from a single sample?

The sharp mind is manifest in the way he has joined every letter together without, as it were, pausing for breath. When writers do this, it means that their thoughts are galloping way ahead of their pens. The Captain has not lifted his from the start of the capital E until he has finished underscoring.

The love of luxury comes through in the garland-type letter connections, which will be explained later. Graphology is so symbolic.

The Captain's love of music is evident in the odd little swirl of his capital E; together with a capital S shaped like a treble clef. This would seem to suggest that he had more than a passing interest in music; he may well have taken an active role, by playing an instrument or two. Perhaps a reader somewhere will be able to confirm whether he did in fact have musical abilities?

Self-importance is seen in the underlined signature. And the sexuality? At this early stage, I shall say simply that the clue is in the inflated loop of the J; but promise to focus more on the erotic aspects of the writers under investigation in later pages.

A couple of other points about the captain before we move on. Family pride and strong devotion to his partner (despite his innocent flirtations with the ladies) is suggested by the fact that his initials and surname are all joined to each other. Like a row of arms linked together.

I note that he has used the initials E. J. rather than his Christian name of Edward. The fact that the initials are of equal size and proportion to the S in Smith, would intimate that he was seldom, if ever known as 'Edward'. It would have been either Captain Smith, or simply EJ : almost as if 'Eejay' were his name and not Edward.

To sum up, therefore, I would describe this signature as harmonious and balanced; showing the writer to be outgoing, sociable, and happy when surrounded by admiring ladies . . . the type of man who might have been described as 'hail fellow, well met'. . .*

It was as a small child that I first encountered graphology. My late father, a doctor, used it in addition to more convential forms of medical diagnosis.

Being a police surgeon, he also found it useful in the field of forensic medicine: helping to detect crime. A nosey little devil, I liked to peer over his shoulder and listen to him voicing his thoughts aloud. My father was a shrewd operator: he also used graphology for personnel selection: by inviting potential receptionists, housekeepers and gardeners to apply in their own handwriting for any jobs that might be going. Had they known what they were letting themselves in for, they might not have bothered applying. But it did seem a foolproof method of ending up with reliable, trustworthy and honest staff.

My father had inherited his fascination for graphology from his father, a prison governor who made a study of criminal hands. Forensic graphology is still used: more widely than the general public probably realise.

The analysis of character from handwriting has many uses. In my former role as Agony Aunt (for the Liverpool Echo and also for IPC's TRUE magazine), the ability to glimpse into the mind of a writer proved invaluable; not only for sorting out which letters were genuine and which were not, but also for getting to the root of readers' problems — sometimes when they were unable to identify those problems themselves.

Tell people you are a graphologist and they look askance. Those who have heard the word assume you are some sort of fortune teller, or guru.

They mistakenly confuse your skills with palmistry, which involves interpreting lines in the hand, and calligraphy, which is the art of creating beautiful scripts with a pen or brush.

It is therefore important at this point to establish what graphology is and what it is not.

IT IS the study of character and personality from handwriting. And that, alone . . .

IT IS NOT for prying into the private thoughts of others; nor is it a party game or cult practice; a means of predicting the future, or in any way connected with tea leaves, tarot cards, astrology or numerology.

The word is of Greek origin — 'grapho' meaning to write or to create symbolic design. Whether it is an art or a science does not really matter; provided the results can be demonstrated. After analysing a page of text, a skilled graphologist should be able to give an accurate image of bodily and mental activity.

By studying an individual's handwriting, the analyst's aim is to evaluate physiological patterns, detect personality traits and behaviour disturbances. An in-depth character assessment is therefore capable of being produced.

Apart from the aspects already mentioned, other interpretations for the use of graphology include career guidance and marriage compatability; though those are two areas which I do not choose to work in myself.

Graphology can also provide insights for those working with disturbed children and adolescents; and it can make an important contribution to the associated fields of medicine and psychology.

Just as X-Rays can penetrate the head to produce clear pictures of the skull, a graphologist's reading can penetrate the writer's thoughts to see what lies behind them, submerged in the unconscious. So, with a few pen strokes, and without even realising what he is doing, the writer can disclose the deep, symbolic meanings of his thoughts.

This is not as outlandish as it seems. Most of our conscious actions are controlled by unconscious mechanisms. The hand may be holding the pen or pencil, but it is the brain which directs the writing instrument around the paper

The most casual observer of handwriting might recognise and identify certain shapes and forms; sort out the flashy from the inhibited; recognise the tidy and untidy; the clever and the slow-witted. But without making a long and protracted study of the subject, these observations are in danger of being too generalised; even inaccurate. If someone's personality is to be completely mapped out, all the features must be taken into consideration. Each must be seen to show a separate relationship in the character as a whole.

Like pieces of a jigsaw, they must all fit into place before the total picture can emerge. We all realise that no two thumb-prints are duplicated, but it may not be so well known that neither are any two handwriting samples: even those of identical twins.

The reason why a graphologist cannot state categorically whether the writing is that of a man or a woman, is because we are all what is known as androgynous creatures: in other words, every female has a certain number of male hormones and every male has female hormones.

And the handwriting will inevitably show signs of each. Enigmatically, although gender cannot be stated for sure, the sexuality — or lack of it — is usually abundantly clear . . .

Where did the idea of graphology originate?

Nobody really knows. Eleventh century Chinese philosophers are believed to have used a form of it. It is claimed, too, that various renowned men of history tried penetrating the personality by this means. Aesop, Aristotle, Caesar, Shakespeare, Sir Walter Scott, Disraeli and Robert Browning are all said to have had a go.

However, the man who really started the ball rolling was Dr. Camillo Baldi, Professor of Theoretical Medicine at the University of Bologna, in the 17th century. He did for the analysis of handwriting what Freud and Jung did for the analysis of the mind. Well, perhaps not quite that . . . but he did bring it out into the open. Like so many other specialist fields, once graphology became acceptable, numerous scientists and doctors took it upon themselves to give it serious consideration and try drawing further connections between personality and writing: but it was not until the 19th century that a possible relationship was seen to exist between physiology, psychology and graphology.

Abbé Hippolyte Michon, who belonged to a French religious order, published a weighty tome on the subject. He it was who introduced the term 'graphology'.

The name has come down into our everyday language. Yet the man who dreamed it up is long forgotten.

---

[6] Another certificate of discharge can be seen in chapter three: it is that of William Faulkner, a first class steward, who also survived the disaster.

[7] There are various reports about the bravery of Captain Smith. Some say he stayed on board, waving to his departing passengers and crew until he went down quietly with his ship; others say he rescued a crying infant, swam with it to a lifeboat, handed it to its mother, but refused a place in the boat himself, preferring to return to his stricken liner; others say it was a dog that he rescued. Whichever story is true, no-one could accuse this man of cowardice: which is more than can be said for Sir Cosmo Duff Gordon (see pages 105-109) and his wife, the lovely Lady Lucy.

HANDS OFF THE TITANIC

CHAPTER TWO:
This was no lady

Chapter Two: This Was No Lady!

Bruce Ismay, managing director of the White Star Line, who owned the Titanic, was no less a 'scapegoat' of the disaster than was Captain Stanley Lord.

All sorts of wild claims were made about him . . . that he ordered Captain Smith to press on at full speed, ignoring all ice warnings in order to set a new world record; that, when the crunch came, he was one of the first off the ship, with all his bags and baggage.

The accusation about his alleged cross-dressing was particularly spurious, considering that Ismay was over six foot tall and moustached. A strange looking woman he would have made. The American newspaper headline which showed a picture of him in a lifeboat, captioned 'This is J. BRUTE Ismay, safe in his lifeboat, while 1500 souls perished' was particularly cruel. It was also totally undeserved.

In fact, like so many other gentlemen on board, Bruce Ismay helped people as much as possible, and only made his escape in one of the last lifeboats. Even then, those who knew him say that he felt horribly guilty about being alive, when, as he kept telling himself for years afterwards, he would have been better off dead. A tortured soul, if ever there was one.

Why, after all, SHOULD he have gone down with his ship? He was a passenger, and a rather important one at that.

Surely as the only director of his company to have witnessed the events of that night, the evidence he might present to the Inquiry into the sinking would be of vital importance. Indeed, it is reliably reported by several passengers and crew that Chief Officer Murdoch actually ordered Ismay into the lifeboat; discreetly reminding him of his duty as a high-ranking official, to speak out.*

History tells us that Ismay went out of his way to help others and that when he finally jumped into the last available boat, there was no-one else around. He was not depriving another passenger of a place: there were 432 unfilled places in the lifeboats leaving Titanic.

Fate did not smile kindly on this man.

After the disaster, he resigned as chairman of the White Star Line. He had, in fact, made the decision to do so BEFORE Titanic's sinking. As Leslie Harrison points out: "His reason was complicated, but was linked with the decision to retire from the chairmanship of International Mercantile Marine, in favour of Harold Sanderson." Bruce Ismay did not become a recluse in Ireland after the disaster, as is generally believed. He continued to live in London, with his American wife, and made frequent visits to Liverpool in connection with his work. He died in 1937.

Figure 2

A cursory glance at his signature, written before the disaster, shows him to be a painfully shy man.

Lofty, inhibited capitals, dominating the middle zone inevitably point to inner conflict. He liked to give the impression of being supremely confident when, in reality, he was the exact opposite.

Bruce Ismay was a mass of complexes.

His writing is narrow, repressed, restricted and full of inhibitions. It is tense, but controlled. All three zones are equally narrow, pointing to a strict upbringing, and a strong sense of duty as a result.

In this sort of hand, politeness and natural reserve are often mistaken for arrogance; but the imperious exterior so often masks a sensitive, easily hurt nature. This man was fiercely independent, and did not find it at all easy to form and sustain relationships. There is, nevertheless, in Bruce Ismay's signature a very materialistic streak.

It is an established graphological fact that when people write letters in the shape of numbers, money matters are foremost in their mind. In this one short signature, we have many such signs.

The B could be said to resemble a 13. The small 'r' is like a 2; the capital I is half way to becoming a nine, and the 'y' resembles a seven. It is an odd signature, to say the least . . .

The acquisition of wealth would appear to have been of prime importance to him — or at least, it was when he penned this particular signature; because graphological assessment can only be based on how the writer is at the actual time of writing.

Analysing a sample of handwriting is a complicated procedure. The graphologist has to examine the sample as a whole; take a long, hard look at it and decide whether it has a natural flow, or is stilted and held back for some reason. The general 'feel' of the writing should be considered: in other words, whether it is regular or irregular, contains any strange letter formations. Size, slant and spacing all have their place in graphological assessment.

The pressure of the writing is something else which is usually very relevant, though with photographs or photocopies of the original, as with most of the samples on these pages, that aspect has had to be overlooked. What does pressure reveal?

The general rule is that the heavier the pressure the more energy expended by the writer. After all, light pen strokes call for considerably less effort than the heavier variety. To continually write with heavy pressure, at speed, demands an abundant supply of energy.

As in speech and dress, we each have our individual style of writing. For some of us, it is much as it was when we were children — slow, painful, tedious. A typical case in point is that of poor Mabel, whoever she was, who wrote the postcard to Master Geoff Moore, featured in Chapter Ten. For others, the pen is like a race horse, galloping along the page (as in the case of William Faulkner, whose writings will be examined in the next chapter.).

Signs of fast writing include a pronounced slant to the right; smooth, unbroken strokes, rounded forms, letters and words joined together; sometimes with i dots and t bars placed high above and to the right of the letter; when i dots are converted to commas, or omitted altogether.

In a very fast hand, i dotting, and punctuation inserting are considered time wasters. (See Captain Bridgewater, in Chapter 12). Slow writing is ornamental, flourishy and contains letters which have been touched up (e.g.. Gibson, Chapter 11 . . . in whose case it appears to have been due mainly to lack of education.). Slow writing can also be a deliberate attempt on the part of the writer to deceive the reader. Or it can be due to a bad pen or paper; ink running out, impaired thought processes, or any one of a number of psychological factors. There might even be a mechanical cause: like an unfamiliar pen, uneven writing surface, an aching wrist, . . . or a sinking ship! . . .

Handwriting is made up of three zones: upper, middle and lower. The upper zones (and their loops) represent the writer's intellect, his imagination, or his high-flown (possibly religious) thoughts. The middle zone tells us something of his general emotional state: the lower focusses on instincts, appetites, sporting and sexual goings-on. 'Leg activities', as I like to call them. An exaggeration of any one zone shows where the writer's main interest lies.

Enlarged upper zones can indicate that the writer is a great thinker; whereas the more practical type — and sports enthusiasts — emphasise the lower. An exaggeration of the middle zones usually comes from writers who are aware of their own attractions (or lack of them), are sociable, and sentimental.

Depending on the shape of them, enlarged lower zones can sometimes indicate materialism.

Writing styles come in five types:

COPYBOOK ANGULAR GARLAND ARCADE THREADY

Figure 3

Copybook shows immaturity, or might even have been adopted as a mask. Angular is usually the work of a cold, quarrelsome individual. Garland reflects a love of luxury.

Arcade comes from people who manage to keep a lid over their emotions. Thready is the work of an indecisive person with low resistance and a wandering mind. And so to line spacing.

Writing which runs up from the baseline denotes enthusiasm, optimism and a happy disposition. Drooping lines hint at tiredness, depression, despondence (as in the later sample of Captain Lord's writing, penned some fifty years after the disaster). Wavering, or disturbed alignment may have serious undertones, as already indicated.

Bear with me for a moment, while we turn back to Bruce Ismay's capital I. Try copying it on to a piece of paper. Now, I ask you . . . how many people would write the letter like that?

In all my years analysing handwriting, I have never, ever, seen an I so written. If Bruce Ismay fashioned his personal pronouns the same way, I would begin to suspect that his boyhood attitudes towards his parents were extremely odd.

I'll explain.

It has already been established that if, in the general text of a person's writing, upper, middle and lower zones harmonise, the indications are that the writer is a harmonious and well-balanced individual. Nowhere is this more clearly seen than in the formation of the personal pronoun.

There should normally be no difference in pressure between the main text and the capital I. We know that a hand of heavy pen pressure usually indicates the writer's high energy and vivacity. If the formation of the I in that hand is particularly strong, a sensuous personality is suggested; although in a heavy hand showing mainly negative traits, it may indicate criminal tendencies. When the I is lighter than the rest of the text, it shows that the writer's self-image is not very strong.

When the personal pronoun slants in a different direction from the rest of the text, watch out for a moody individual. And when it is written in reverse, then the writer is a very awkward sort of person, indeed. (How to determine whether it has been written with reversed strokes: note which end of the letter is heavy, to suggest its starting point and then see where it tails off).

Real revelations emerge from the personal pronoun. In graphology, it is the classic 'ego symbol'.

It is generally accepted that the top part of the letter relates to the 'mother' and the lower parts to 'father'; or, more precisely, the influence on the writer of mother (or mother substitute) and father (or father substitute). A discrepancy between the two shows the discrepancy between the effect each parent had on the subject being analysed.

Fig.
4

—→   MOTHER INFLUENCE

——→   FATHER INFLUENCE

The personal pronoun takes on as many shapes and forms as the writers who produce it. It would take a whole book to explain them all, and the details have no place in a work of this nature. Reference to the personal pronoun I is made only so that, realising the fact this this symbol does figure so prominently in psychographology, readers may understand some of the conclusions drawn in the following pages. So, if Bruce Ismay's PPI WERE the same as the I in his surname, one might be inclined to conclude that he had tried hard, but without success, to be warm and friendly towards his mother, but for reasons best known to himself,severed the ties with his father at a very early age.

This type of cut-off on the bottom of the personal pronoun is often seen in the handwriting of those whose fathers demanded standards so high that they simply could not be achieved

They would, as a result, be accompanied by signs pointing to shyness and inadequacy; similar to those seen in Ismay's signature.

The signature is the stamp of our personality and how we project ourselves to others: the public image, the giving of autographs. The page of text represents inner feelings. Where they differ, it means the writer is presenting one image to the public at large, but another to those sharing his private life.

Having armed you with all this information, allow me now to escort you on a highly individual guided tour of the Titanic.

In 1988, my daughter Esther (who lives near Göthenberg) visited the Titanic Exhibition at the National Maritime Museum in Stockholm and introduced herself to Claes-Göran Wetterholm, the man who mounted it. After extensive research into the fate of Nordic passengers, Claes-Göran wrote a book about the Titanic (see page 54); the first to be published in Swedish since 1912. Then he read an early draft of this one.

He took issue with a few of my points. (About Ismay, he observed: "It is extremely doubtful if Murdoch ordered Ismay into the lifeboat. Ismay didn't see anybody around and so stepped into lifeboat C. No-one could grasp the enormity of the situation. Ismay probably believed that most women were saved."

His opinion on Captain Smith also differed from mine) but then, as he said: "With so much interst in the case of the Titanic, it seems that today the only thing we can all agree on is that she sank."

HANDS OFF THE TITANIC

CHAPTER THREE:

A First Class Steward

Chapter Three: A First Class Steward

In this chapter, I would like to focus attention on just one man . . . William Faulkner, first class steward. And a first class seaman he was too, as we shall see.

To start at the beginning. William Faulkner lived in Mounsey Road, Birkenhead, with his wife Sybil (a former governess) and their three small children. Having served for some years on the s.s. Celtic, he, like so many other seafarers, considered the Titanic one of the most beautiful creations ever designed by man; so was thrilled and honoured to sail on her trials from Belfast in March 1912.

His happiness was complete when told he was also one of the hand-picked crew chosen to serve on the magnificent floating palace during her maiden voyage a month later. Faulkner, assigned to shelter deck C; the most luxurious of all, watched its cabins filling up with the cream of British and American society, and felt proud to be associated with such internationally famous celebrities. How enchanted his little family would be to hear about all this when he returned to Cheshire. He would be the envy of all his mates too, for it was no secret that many seamen would give their eye teeth to have gone on that trip. They would readily have swopped places to serve on her. Faulkner's wages for the entire trip were a mere £2. 7s 6d; but that hardly bothered him.

The attractions of these sort of duties could not be measured in financial terms. It would never have occured to him to think about any discrepancies. Nor would he have been likely to dwell on the social injustices attached to the fact that, while his earnings were so paltry, the passengers in his care were mainly millionaires. In 1912, those sort of issues simply did not arise.

The names of many of the passengers were already legendary: Astor, Guggenheim, Rothschild, Ryerson, Widener; complete with wives, children, maids, men servants. Some had even brought along their pampered pooches. Most were American, though there were a few British and other international celebrities . . . artists, painters, writers and the like.

Stewards were all given their printed lists of names. Faulkner read the words 'First Class Passenger list, per Royal and US Mail'. The staterooms of those for whom he had responsibility had been ticked with a pencil mark by Chief Purser Herbert McElroy:

First the even numbers -C.42, Graham, Mr.; C.46, Cavendish, Mr. and Mrs. T.W. and maid; C.54, Hays, Miss Margaret.

Then the odd numbers -C.7, Bonnell, Miss Caroline; C.45, Endres, Miss Caroline; C.47, Marechal, M. Pierre; C.49, Isham, Miss A.E.; C.51, Gracie, Col. Archibald; C.53, Earnshaw, Miss Boulton and

Tucker, Mr. G.M. Jnr.; C.55, Straus, Mr. Isidor and manservant; C.57, Straus, Mrs. Isidor and maid.

Into C51, Steward Faulkner — brown eyed and so handsome in his White Star uniform — led the colonel; and into the nearby C55, the elderly Straus couple. A fellow steward opened the door of the large and very plush C62 to usher in the wealthiest passengers aboard.

Colonel John Jacob Astor was accompanied by his teenaged bride who looked young enough to be his daughter. There had been something of a scandal surrounding this couple. Colonel Astor had offended against society by divorcing his wife of many years to marry this pretty young girl at his side. The Astors had enjoyed an extended honeymoon in Egypt and Europe, and were now returning home: at last, they hoped, to escape the packs of newshounds who seemed intent on following them everywhere.

Chief Purser McElroy suddenly appeared at Faulkner's side. He was accompanied by a passenger who wanted a cabin other than that allocated. Mr. Howard B. Case, an oil magnate with interests on both sides of the Atlantic, had been given accommodation down on E deck, and he was none too pleased. He had specifically asked for C and wanted to switch cabins, even if it meant sacrificing space.

The purser had found one more to Mr. Case's liking; handed the steward his note of authorisation for the changeover and asked him to attend to the matter. Faulkner read the note, pocketed it and carried out the instruction. Another happy passenger.

The steward resumed his patrol of the deck; ensuring that all of them were comfortable, and that they lacked for nothing. And so, the great ship set sail . . . .

On hearing the impact, and knowing — or perhaps just sensing — serious trouble, Faulkner checked all the cabins on his list to ensure that no-one was trapped inside. In the course of his rounds, he bumped into a children's nanny, carrying a baby.

She was distraught. The child's mother was missing, she explained. Would he mind holding it briefly, while she searched for her mistress? William Faulkner said that no, of course, he would not mind. He took the crying infant from her, placated it and clung to it until he could no longer guarantee its safety. Despite an extensive search, he never saw the nanny again. The child's mother was nowhere to be found either, so he placed the little one carefully in the arms of a woman being eased into one of the lifeboats. There must have been several very confused infants and toddlers that night. Like so many blanketed parcels, small children were being passed around to anyone prepared to take them. As the crisis became increasingly severe, Faulkner's main duty was to ensure that all the women and children were wearing life-jackets before being ejected from the now-rapidly sinking ship.

31

When all the boats had been lowered, and there was no sign of any more passengers left, crew members still aboard heard the voice of their master call out that from here on it was now a case of 'every man for himself' . . . .

During those bitterly cold hours spent in the lifeboat on the black waters of the Atlantic, William Faulkner thought of Sybil and the children, and prayed he would see them again. The long night passed.

Safely aboard the rescue ship Carpathia, he found he had just three items in his pocket. They were: the printed list of passengers in his care, the purser's handwritten note requesting Mr. Case's transfer, and a key to cabin number 24, complete with tag, allowing its occupant access to a first class bathroom.

Colonel Gracie, one of his 'own' passengers, survived the sinking, but never recovered from the effects of it. Nevertheless, he recorded all his experiences and his emotions on paper, and his book about the disaster sold well. Sadly, Colonel Gracie did not live long enough to see himself in print.*[8]

William Faulkner was summoned to the official inquiry in London, which he attended with his fellow survivors from the crew. Of those on this steward's passenger list, the majority of the men were lost, though most of their wives, children and maid servants were saved. Mrs. Madeleine Astor was widowed after only a few short months of marriage. Mr. Graham was lost; the Cavendish family and their maid were saved, as were Miss Hays and Miss Endres. So was Monsieur Marechal, but poor Miss Isham was lost. Mrs. Earnshaw and young Master Tucker were saved. Whether Mr. Case's cabin move was motivated by feelings of foreboding, neither William Faulkner, nor anyone else could say, for he lost his life in the tragedy. When last seen, he was helping a group of ladies into a lifeboat.

While many of the wives were saved, Mrs. Isidor Straus was one notable exception. Refusing to leave the husband she loved more than life itself, the old lady had gone to the sea bed with him. They were last seeing sitting side by side on deck chairs; proud and dignified as they waited for the end . . . .

Psychologists say that the only way to recover from a car crash is to get straight back into the driving seat and not allow the fear of the vehicle to put you off for life. The same theory applies to horses and aeroplanes. And, of course, ships.

So William Faulkner did what he considered best for himself and all concerned: after a suitable period of grieving and offering his condolences to the bereaved, he returned to work: initially on the s.s. Adriatic (in June, 1912), then on a whole host of other ships, until finally, his bosses had to ask him to retire from the Britannic . . . by which time, he was in his seventies. (There was also a practical reason for his return to duty: his wages, like those of every member of Titanic's crew, stopped the moment the ship sank).

However, the events of that April night in 1912 remained with him all his life. He had lost many friends and fellow crew members in the disaster. He had seen men, women and children die all around him.

As a family man, he had been profoundly shocked to see so many young people lose their lives, and to know that he was powerless to help them. A quiet, reserved person, he seldom spoke about the events of that night in 1912. And who could blame him?

To his grand-daughter, Mrs. Patricia Andrews, he was a wonderful man. During the eleven years she knew and loved him, his homecomings were the highlight of her young life. He would bring her gifts of money, biscuits, chocolates, tinned and dried fruit; which, in those days of rationing, thrilled and delighted Patricia and her two brothers.

Mrs. Andrews treasures the memories of her grandfather's long seafaring life, and protects the many mementoes like the Crown Jewels.

It is thanks to Mrs. Andrews that I am able to reproduce a few of them here . . . as follows:-

* A picture postcard, captioned, 'Launch of the giant White Star liner, Titanic, Belfast, May 31 , 1911. Largest vessel in the world.' And on the back, William's message of love for his wife. *(Figure 5)*

* Stereotyped letter requesting his attendance at the Board of Trade inquiry. *(Figure 6)*

* Extract from his official papers, with the poignant message stating that the original book was lost through shipwreck. *(Figure 7)*

The writing on the postcard is that of a man of high intelligence. The writer's mind works at such a speed that it is running way ahead of his hand, as proved by the way certain words are joned to each other by a single stroke — 'both my', 'to morrow', 'to all'. To this sort of writer, pen lifting is associated with time-wasting and time-wasting formed no part of William Faulkner's makeup.

The general flow of the writing, with its beautifully shaped letters show him to have been artistic.

The occasional appearance of Greek-style letters ('e' in 'love'; 'd' in 'Road') point to literary ability. Capitals D and S formed like musical symbols denote talent in that area too. A certain flamboyance is also evident . . . how else could one describe that 'B' in 'Birkenhead'? The rightward slant shows a cheery, friendly nature, but the wide, inter-word spacing indicates that this steward knew his place.

He kept his distance from his peers, but he was remarkably close to his wife. Note how the gap between 'dearest' and 'Sybil' is less than half that between the words 'got' and 'both' on the next line.

33

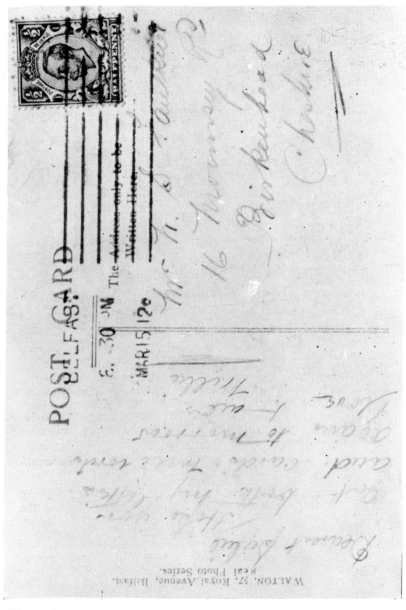

Figure 5

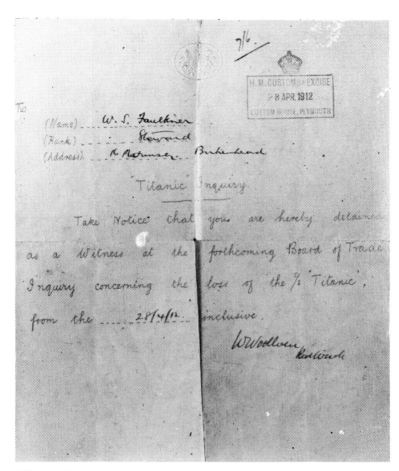

Figure 6

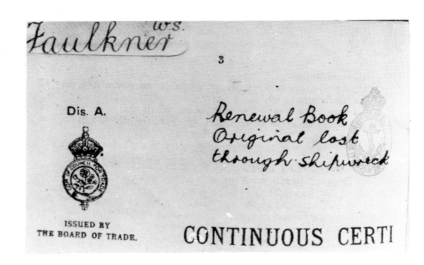

Figure 7

All told, at this stage in his life, he was a happy, carefree young man, full of the joys of springtime and wildly enthusiastic about his forthcoming trip . . . .

There is little a graphologist can glean from the note signed by W. Woolven, the then local Receiver of Wrecks and Collector of Customs at Plymouth, other than to assume that it was not Mr. Woolven himself who filled in the details at the top of the notice. The two styles of writing are quite different.

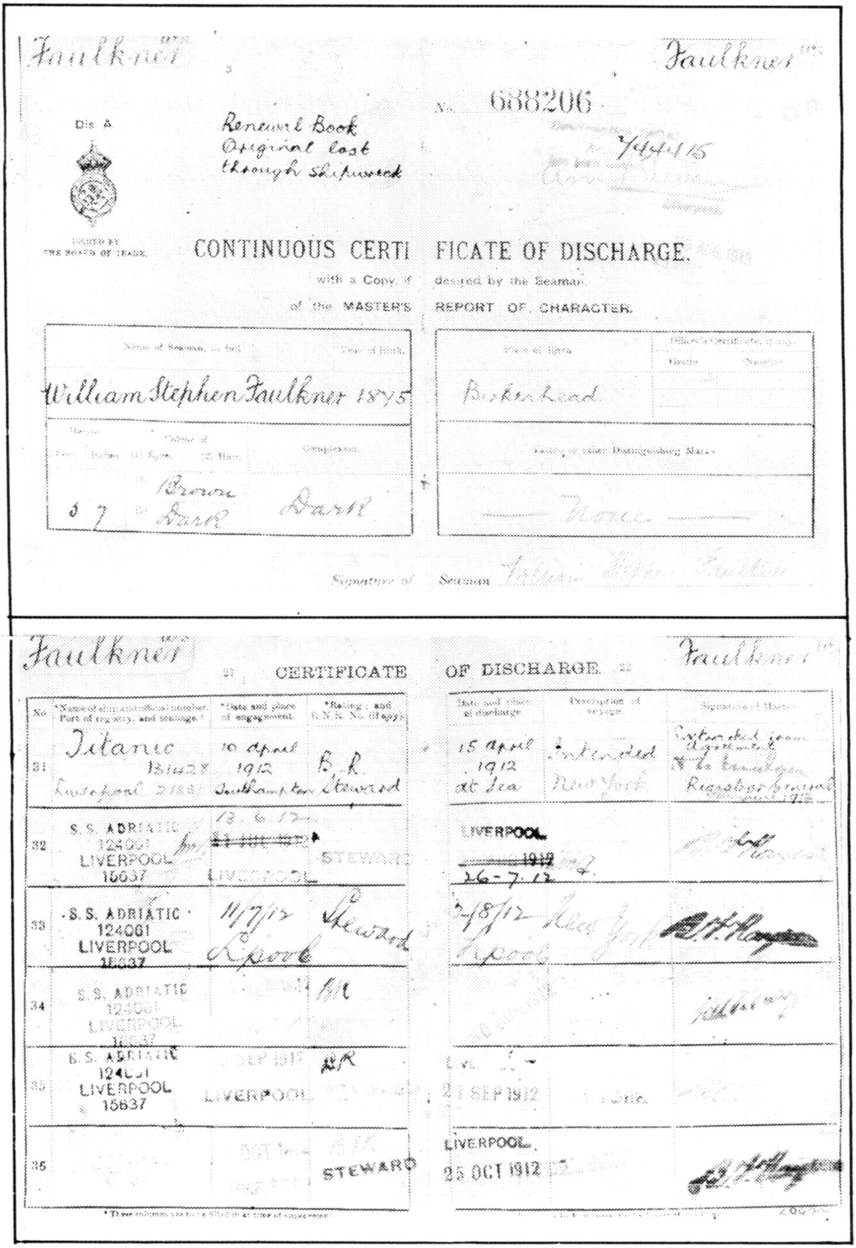

Faulkner | Faulkner

No. 688206

Dis. A

Renewal Book
Original lost
through Shipwreck

7/4/15

ISSUED BY
THE BOARD OF TRADE.

CONTINUOUS CERTIFICATE OF DISCHARGE.

with a Copy, if desired by the Seaman,

of the MASTER'S REPORT OF CHARACTER.

Name of Seaman, in full	Year of Birth	Place of Birth	Officer's Certificate, if any: Grade	Number
William Stephen Faulkner	1875	Birkenhead		

Height: Feet	Inches	Colour of (1) Eyes	(2) Hair	Complexion	Tattoo or other Distinguishing Marks
5	7	(1) Brown	(2) Dark	Dark	None

Signature of Seaman William Stephen Faulkner

Faulkner | CERTIFICATE OF DISCHARGE | Faulkner

No.	*Name of ship and official number, Port of registry, and tonnage.*	*Date and place of engagement.*	*Rating; and R.N.R. No. (if any).*	Date and place of discharge	Description of voyage	Signature of Master
31	Titanic 131428 Liverpool 21831	10 April 1912 Southampton	B.R. Steward	15 April 1912 at Sea	Intended New York	Extracted from agreement to Registrar General
32	S.S. ADRIATIC 124061 LIVERPOOL 15637	13-6-12 LIVERPOOL	STEWARD	LIVERPOOL 1912 26-7-12		[illegible]
33	S.S. ADRIATIC 124061 LIVERPOOL 15637	11/7/12 L'pool	Steward	2/8/12 L'pool	New York	[illegible]
34	S.S. ADRIATIC 124061 LIVERPOOL 15637		B/R			[illegible]
35	S.S. ADRIATIC 124061 LIVERPOOL 15637	5 SEP 1912 LIVERPOOL	B/R	27 SEP 1912	New York	
36		OCT 1912	B/R STEWARD	LIVERPOOL 25 OCT 1912		[illegible]

* These columns are to be filled in at time of engagement.

Figure 8

The tiny script in the top left hand corner is that of a writer who seems to have penned so many of these that he (she?) is on the point of developing writer's cramp — a very real clinical condition, where, at its worst, the hand actually trembles, then siezes up. Note the stumbling over the word 'Mounsey', and the taut execution of the word 'Birkenhead'.

Whoever penned the note saying 'Renewal book — original lost through shipwreck' did not have much of a personality. Bored and boring, this is the work of a dismal 'pen pusher' . . . a little man, with a strong sense of self importance.

With its emphasis on the middle zone, it has come from a writer who has few interests outside him (her?) self. It is negative and untidy . . . note the ink blobs appearing all over the place. This writer is heavy handed in more ways than one . . . bad tempered (thick, pasty script), secretive (closed o's, combined with blacked out upper loops) and immature. Generally speaking, it is as negative as William Faulkner's writing is positive.

Which brings us back to the man himself (see discharge note).

It is a chastened William Stephen Faulkner who signed this certificate in 1913. Sixteen months after his ordeal, he is rather less flamboyant than he was when he wrote the postcard.

For a start, those ornate, curly S's have become much more basic. To find out why they should do that, we must resort to symbolism, as is so often necessary in psycho-graphology: and work it out almost as we might a mathematical equation. If 's' equals 'ship' and 'ship' equals 'Titanic', then in march 1912, to Faulkner, the image conjured up in his mind was one of style and grandeur. A year later, the same symbol would naturally evoke a much more sombre image. If 's' still equalled 'ship', it would no longer conjure up pictures of the Titanic, but of other more mundane vessels. Therefore, the letter itself, would take on a more basic shape. As the mathematicians might say, Q.E.D.

Even his signature appears more subdued than before. Note that the underscore has now vanished, and with it (at least in his own mind), the status.

Purser McElroy's note will be analysed in chapter seven, alongside the writings of other members of the Titanic crew. Sadly, the purser was not among the survivors.

*8 Titanic, A Survivor's Story, by Colonel Archibald Gracie, Alan Sutton Publishing, 1985 (first published, 1913).

HANDS OFF THE TITANIC

CHAPTER FOUR:

Captain Lord, the real story

Chapter Four: Captain Lord — The Real Story

It is strange how people's foibles can be reflected in their writing.

Sometimes, I am called upon to examine two or more samples of handwriting for the purpose of stating whether they might have been written by the same person. Colleagues have asked me to compare genuine letters with alleged forgeries. Business executives have invited me to cast an eye over two apparently different styles of writing coming from what was believed to be the same person.

The editor of a popular Sunday newspaper once presented me with two very similar handwritten notes, penned by different writers. He thought he had stumbled across something unusual, but in fact, this is quite a common occurence when one person moulds himself (herself) on another. An impressive teenager might copy the style of a more dominant older person; likewise a relatively unknown stage or TV performer with a more famous one. Even Royalty have been known to do it, as we shall see. It is quite fascinating to compare the strengths of one with the weaknesses of the other.

Recently, a very rare case was brought to my notice. It was that of a man in his thirties who had five or six (known) writing styles; though there may well have been more. They were as different from each other as any I had ever seen — in size, slant, angle and even letter structure. They reflected the many personalities he projected to those around him. This man had, of course, a severe personality disorder.

I mention his case only in passing, to illustrate how the state of our mind can affect the way we write . . . .

Changes in handwriting can occur after illness, injury, or some extremely emotional event. Nelson's writing looked quite different after his right arm was blown off and he had to learn to write with his left, though the basic outlines remained constant, as they always would in such circumstances, because it is in the brain that the control area is sited.

Hence the changes in writing which inevitably take place after mental illness, injury or trauma. Changes of psychological origin are influenced by the state of the writer's mind. 'Banana slips' do not just happen on the pavement, they can also occur on a page of script.

When individual words and their associated thoughts stand out in the text, they do so for a reason. Without thinking, the writer has met an obstacle and has paused, tried to bypass, but instead, has accentuated or even tripped over it. This subconscious stumbling can tell much about the thoughts of the writer. A slip of the pen can be as revealing as a slip of the tongue.

That sort of unconscious activity can be very helpful to the analyst: not only when certain letters or words dominate a page, but also when they pale into obscurity or are missing altogether. Their absence means that, deep in his mind, the writer believes the letters or words irrelevant to his thinking: they have an unpleasant association, or they represent an issue he is trying to avoid.

Such psychological hiccoughs must appear regularly for them to have significance. If they only show up once or twice, it could be because the pen has run out of ink, the pencil's lead has broken, someone has interrupted the writer's flow of thoughts, or for any one of a number of reasons. The regular occurence of an unusual formation must be taken more seriously . . . .

I promised earlier that I would say something about how a person's sensuality and sexuality can be reflected in the writing. Sensuality shows itself in heavy pressure; particularly when applied to the downstrokes. In that sort of hand, sensuality shows itself in the lower zones of the g and y. They are usually looped and large.

The smaller their lower loops, the less the sex drive. Cut-off lower loops suggest repression and those which swing to the right, rather than to the left en route for the baseline, hint at inhibitions in early life, possibly due a a strong 'father influence'. Tension, depression and neurotic tendencies might be suggested by long, narrow loops; tiny little stick loops point to sexual inadequacy and neglected underloops suggest that physical desire is virtually non-existent.

Criminality can also be detected from a person's writing. The classical signs are varying slant, over-embellished capitals, the touching up of letters, missing letters, a script which is half written, half printed, blacked out letters, and so on . . . .

It is useful to know some basic facts about dishonesty and deceit when considering an analysis of Captain Lord's handwriting **PURELY FOR THE PURPOSE OF ELIMINATION.**

Stanley Lord was Captain of the Californian; the man who reputedly slept in his bunk while his officers stood on the bridge of their ship watching the Titanic send up distress signals for help and did nothing.

Lord was unjustly charged with being responsible for the loss of 1500 lives. He insisted his ship was never close enough to the Titanic to render assistance to passengers before she sank. A schooner had been sighted in the area. And it was known that at least one poacher (illegally hunting seals) was also nearby. There were several ships in those waters on the night in question, other than the Titanic, the Californian and the Carpathia; but then it is no secret that books and films often sell better if the truth is 'embellished' and the complications removed.

Captain Lord was never given a chance to defend himself against the accusations. The unfortunate man felt a sense of outrage at the damage done to his professional and personal reputation, as well he might.

His professional history shows him to have been a first-rate officer. At 23, he gained his extra master's certificate; at 24 he became a chief officer; at 29 he was appointed master of a passenger cargo liner and at the time of the 'Californian Incident', he was still only 35.

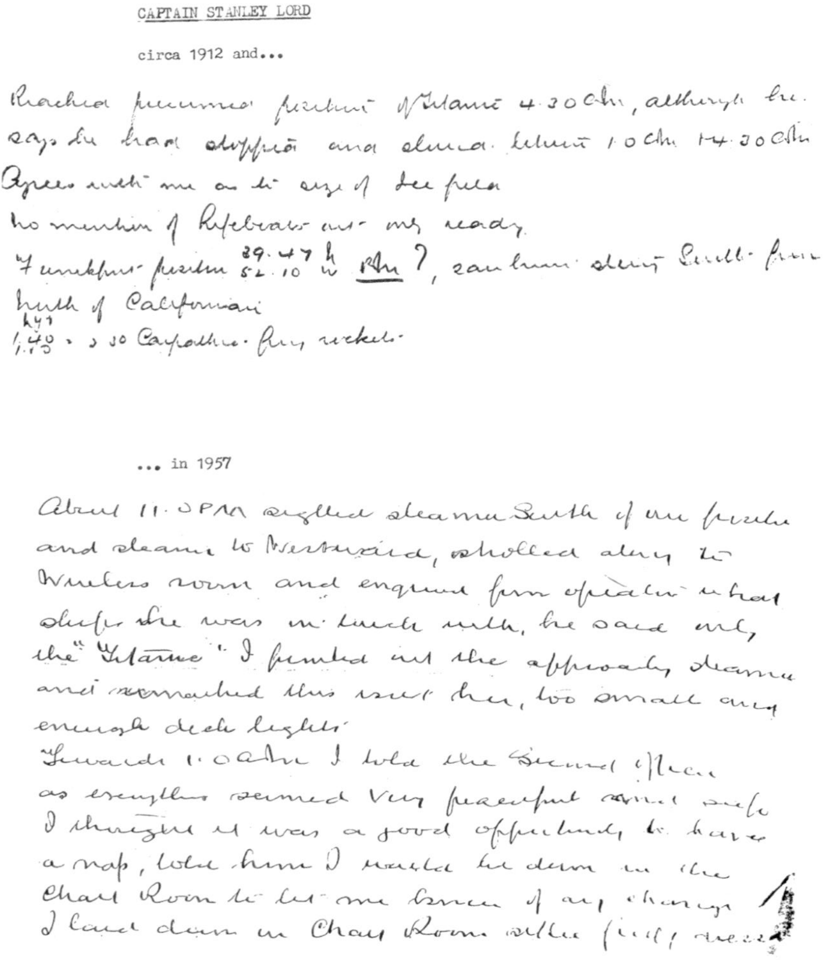

CAPTAIN STANLEY LORD

circa 1912 and...

Reached presumed position of Titanic 4.30 am, although he says he had stopped and drifted between 1.0 am & 4.30 am
Agrees with me as to size of ice field
No mention of lifeboats [illegible] ready.
7 [illegible] position 39.47 N 52.10 W 8 am ?, saw him steering South from North of Californian
1.40 – 2.30 Carpathia firing rockets.

... in 1957

About 11.0 PM sighted steamer South of our position and steaming to Westward, strolled along to Wireless room and enquired from operator what ships he was in touch with, he said only the "Titanic". I pointed out the approaching steamer and remarked this isn't her, too small and not enough deck lights.
Towards 1.0 am I told the Second Officer as everything seemed very peaceful and safe I thought it was a good opportunity to have a nap, told him I would be down in the Chart Room to let me know of any change. I laid down in Chart Room settee fully dressed

Figure 9

In comparing Captain Lord's two samples of writing, we are not just examining what changes might have come about in the intervening forty five years between samples (a) and (b) as a straightforward contrast between the writing of someone who is aged thirty five and aged eighty. In this most unique case, we are also having to compare the writing of a ship's master giving an account of a disastrous event in his professional life, with providing a hindsight account of that same tragic event, now in the light of a totally unexpected and undeserved slur on both his personal and professional reputations.

Captain Lord was guilty of no crime.

There is not a trace of criminality in either of these samples. On the contrary, there is much warmth, humanity and understanding to be seen. Naturally, his writing and therefore his attitudes and outlook, have changed over the years. Whose would not, in the circumstances? He had — to use a modern idiom — been 'traumatised'. But there is nothing sinister to be found in either sample.

The dominant theme to come through from both samples is the strength of the man: his refusal to be compromised in any way: or bullied into submission.

As we change, so does our handwriting. That is only to be expected and is perfectly natural. As our character changes, we think — and therefore, we write — differently.

But how many of us would retain the same writing style over forty five years?

It takes an enormous amount of internal stability to produce identical scripts with so many years apart. Yet, amazingly, Captain Lord manages to do it. This, I feel, is very significant.

Both samples are smooth, flowing and utterly lacking in tasteless flourish or ornamentation, although it has to be said that both samples are also narrow. They could be described as repressed, restricted and full of inhibitions . . . which is perfectly natural in the circumstances. This, after all, was a proud man, a leader, trained not to reveal his emotions. The writing is tense, but controlled. The script is tall, thin and stands upright, denoting politeness and natural reserve . . . even, as in the case of Bruce Ismay, with those narrow capitals, providing a hint of shyness.

Many of the letters have looped stems, particularly in the later sample, showing how deeply he had been wounded; they show too, his ability to keep that 'stiff upper lip' and not give in to pressures from those who thought they knew his business better than he. This writing also shows a strong sense of duty. The words are fairly well separated, so the safe assumption is that here was an independent man who did not find it easy to form and sustain relationships outside his immediate family. Perhaps if he had been more of a 'jolly tar' and socialised with influential people of the day, the outcome might have been different: but that was not Captain Lord's style.

His writing in 1912 was a shade more imperious than in 1957; the giveaway sign being the formation of the 'm' in the earlier sample. (A high first stem, 'lording it' over the two much smaller ones). Looped stems appear more frequently in the later sample, confirming the observation about his having been wounded by the slur on both his professional judgement and his personal character.

In 1912, his personal pronouns are all more or less the same. At that time, he was quite sure of himself and knew in his heart that he was right.

Over the years, however, he apparently had some sort of identity crisis, because those I's now vary tremendously in shape and size:-

'I told second officer' (the I is tiny and compressed)
'I would lie down' (that I is perfectly open and honest:
  it is part of a statement of fact)
'I laid down' (remembering that, he reverts to a very primitive
  form of the letter . . . almost as if, by now, he is beginning to lose
  heart).

Now for a really quirky sign: those double loops at the top of the capital T, which are a dominant feature in the later sample, but are not present at all in the former (though the capital F does display a rather similar characteristic, which is entirely irrelevant).

What do the double loops mean? In simple terms, they show that the writer stumbles when he begins to write the word Titanic — and for that matter, most other words commencing with capital T. This is what I call a mental 'banana slip'; only, unlike the pavement variety which only occasionally appear, these regularly crop up.

They show us how very deeply he was affected by the circumstances surrounding the Titanic disaster. Captain Lord might not have consciously realised this; but graphology is concerned with the subconscious, not the conscious, mind. In analysing handwriting, the graphologist must penetrate the one to reach the other.

And the capital F in the 1912 sample? This bears no relationship to the Titanic, or to any part of his professional duties, so forgive me if I bypass it and return to the analysis of the 1957 sample. The many changes of pressure indicate increasing frailty of his body; though his mind is still very alert. By now, we see also that he appears to have been suffering from failing eyesight (the increasingly large letter formations) and to be a trifle hard of hearing (some of the 'I's have gone ear-shaped — simplistic though it may seem, that is quite a giveaway).

44

The conclusions to be drawn from the comparison — which was in fact very much more extensive that I have been able to reproduce here — is that this man was no criminal.

More to the point, let us hear from the Captain' son, also named Stanley Lord. Having been presented with the foregoing analysis of his father's writing, this is what he said:-

"My father always used to maintain that the light seen from the Titanic approaching and then receding into the distance could not have been from the Californian as she was stationary from approximately 10.00 p.m. until 6.00 a.m., when she set off on the two and a half hour journey, through massive ice-fields, to where Titanic went down.

"My father was teetotal and the innuendo contained in a remark of Rufus Isaacs at the Inquiry that it did not do to enquire too closely into what was going on in the chartroom that night, implying that father was drunk, annoyed him intensely. He wrote to Isaacs, but received a reply that he was out of the country and that no correspondence was being forwarded. The mud stuck.

"In your analysis of father's handwriting, you suggest that it shows deep, psychological trauma, loss of self esteem and depression.

"You must remember that he was over eighty years of age when that letter was written and with a cataract forming on one eye (later removed satisfactorily) and a somewhat shaky hand, I feel he did very well.

"As for self-esteem; whilst he was always a very retiring and un-flamboyant person, he most certainly never lost his self-esteem."

Mr. Lord did make the point that his mother had been dead then only a matter of months after a very long illness, during which his father cared for her with great love and attention. Her death left him utterly shattered.

"I attribute the depression you have detected to that and that alone."

I never knew Captain Lord personally; though it could be debated that, through analysing his writing, I have a deeper knowledge of him than if we had actually met.

I have, however, had the privilege of meeting Mr. Stanley Lord, his son.

Mr. Lord was kind enough to give me an afternoon of his valuable time when I began researching this book. He located all sorts of memorabilia for me — photographs, letters, passports, the deeds of his father's house. He spoke of his father's great love for his family. The captain and his wife were devoted to animals; a love their only son has inherited.

Figure 10

Figure 11

Figure 12

Figure 13

Those who did not know him, who pointed their filth-encrusted fingers at him, had the gall to describe this wonderful man as 'unapproachable' and 'an autocrat'. What absolute rubbish.

As I sat in the high-backed leather chair in the dining room of Mr. Lord's home and listened, enchanted, to him rolling back the years, it was as if time had collapsed.

Mr. Lord recalled many incidents relating to his father's bravery and compassion; one of which occured when he was captain of the Anglo Chilean (his last ship before retiring).

He risked his own life to save that of one of his crew who had fallen down the hold. Frank John Goodchild was an apprentice and his captain was the first person to reach him. He lifted the boy up and heard him utter the words 'Sorry, Sir' before lapsing into unconsciousness. Goodchild recovered from his injuries and subsequently became a lifelong friend of Captain Lord and his family. Another indication of Captain Lord's compassion comes through in his devotion to animals.

"Many years ago" recalled his son "We had a beautiful dog; a cross Labrador Airedale called Jerry. I grew up with Jerry and we all three loved him.

"When the dog became terminally ill through old age, father wrapped him in a rug and took him to the vet, who advised him to let the dear old boy go. Father sat with him and held his paw until he had gone. When he returned home he said, 'I cried a bit then, you know'."

Thirty four years later, when the Captain himself was nearing death, the memory of that dog was still fresh in his mind.

His dying thoughts were of his long-lost friend.

'Ah . . . dear old Jerry . . . he was one of the family.' he said, then added quietly 'I think I will go home now.' Then he made himself comfortable and drifted peacefully into his last sleep.

Here, then, was a man with real depth of feeling; but a man who, because of his outwardly reserved nature, was not inclined to display those feelings in public. The idea of his refusing to help hundreds of people in trouble is ludicrous.

Would such a man be likely to turn his back on hundreds of people about to lose their lives in the greatest shipping disaster the world has ever known? Of course he would not.

His son said so in a television programme commemorating the 50th Anniversay of the sinking. Asked if Captain Lord would have gone to rescue the Titanic immediately had he realised she was in trouble, his son responded that the captain would have rescued a tugboat if he had thought it was in danger.

Figure 14

For reasons best known to themselves, certain members of Lord's crew turned on him. Money passed hands: evidence was twisted. The issue was clouded by personal resentment: who knows what really did happen on that night of nights?

All I can say, having examined the writings of Captain Lord, is that the fault most certainly did not lie with him.

"The Titanic was on the eastern side of the ice belt" explained his son "and the Californian was on the western side. Father did not know anything about the Titanic until next morning and his ship was so far away from the disaster site that it took him two and a half hours **IN DAYLIGHT** to arrive there. He passed certain other ships on the way. The movements of one were highly suspect, but its captain was exonerated."

Leyland Line management in Liverpool never did believe the charges against Captain Lord but, on instructions from the Board of Directors in London, they could not continue to employ him. Thankfully, one man was still in a position to help. That was Sir John Latta, chairman of Lawther Latta, the shipping company.

Explains Mr. Lord:

"From the first meeting with father, Sir John appeared to regard him as entirely reliable and trustworthy; so much so that when his last and largest ship came out, he gave him command of the vessel, although he was then the youngest captain in the firm."

Sir John's trust in Captain Lord never faltered. When the Anglo-Chilean was preparing for her maiden voyage from Sunderland to the Clyde during the First World War, with Captain Lord in command, the captain wrote to Sir John for his opinion. This ship, after all, was about to enter very dangerous waters.

"The U-Boat menace was at its height and the route lay around the north of Scotland where HMS Hampshire was sunk en route for Russia."

Sir John's reply was most gratifying and greatly appreciated by its recipient. He told the captain to 'deal with the ship exactly as if she were your own property'.

Not surprisingly, Captain Lord and Sir John frequently discussed the Titanic incident and Sir John was heard to observe:

"Well, Captain, if you had been in command of one of my ships on that occasion, you would not have been sacrificed to public opinion as you were then.'.

Captain Lord served throughout the First World War and honourably since.

His death occured just a few months before the 50th Anniversary of Titanic's sinking.

Rumours were then circulated that he had died of drink: a frustrated and unhappy man: penniless, in the slums of London.

Much as certain antagonists and authors of popular works of fiction might like to substantiate the rumours, the fact is that Captain Lord did nothing of the sort. It is to his credit that he retained his self-respect and his dignity to the end.

His conscience was clear. The slander, intrigue and personal differences could no longer affect him.

How happy it would have made him to have had his name cleared officially before he breathed his last. Sadly, it was not to be.

For the sake of history and in the cause of justice, I truly believe that, having probed the mind of this man, the stigma attached to Captain Lord should be removed, albeit posthumously and his case vindicated.

More importantly, so does Leslie Harrison who, because of his post at the MMSA (detailed in prologue) and being a master mariner himself, was in a unique position to study the tragic dilemma of the man he grew to know and respect.

Mr. Harrison, who has written a comprehensive account, based on the captain's contemporary papers and later reminiscences, told me:

"The findings of the judicial inquiry constitute the grossest miscarriage of justice in the history of British Inquiries."

Subsequent attempts to rectify the situation have all proved fruitless . . . but as long as there are people alive who feel strongly about Captain Lord, the fight to clear his name will go on. I hope it never ceases until somebody, somewhere, takes it upon themselves to redress the balance. After all, this was a man maligned above all others . . . a man who was absolutely innocent of crime; as his handwriting has proved.

All of this begs the question . . . if the ship seen by the Titanic was not the Californian and that seen by the Californian was not the Titanic, were they both looking at some other vessels somewhere between them? Yes, apparently, they were.

"Two other ships were involved." Leslie Harrison points out "the one seen from the Titanic and another seen from the Californian."

It seems possible that the ship seen from the Titanic could have been a Norwegian sealer, named Samson. Though much speculation surrounds the events of that night, Samson's first officer, Henrik Naess did subsequently admit to having been in the vicinity at the time.

Naess actually submitted a report to the Norwegian Consul in April 1912, in which he stated that on the night of the disaster, he saw 'two big stars' which turned out to be 'lanterns and lots of lights'. He further added that moments later, he noticed several rockets. Then all the lights disappeared.

Samson was a small wooden ship, primarily occupied in killing seals. It had no wireless aboard, so could not have intercepted distress messages. Naess' report continues:

'The Samson's position was such that it feared we might be taken for violating territorial waters and there were Americans in the neighbourhood. When the lights went out this probably meant we were being observed; the rockets being, maybe, signals to other ships. We therefore changed course and hurried northwards.

When dawn came, there was no sign of ships anywhere.'

Author Richard Garrett, puts it:

'The Samson slunk away like a thief in the night.'

He goes on to suggest that when, on arriving in Iceland, Naess learned of the Titanic disaster, he checked his log and discovered that the date, time and position co-incided with his own observations.

'But the Norwegian Consul thought it best to keep this information to themselves. The report was not made public until 1962, by which time Captain Lord was dead. Had they spoken out at the time, the name of Captain Lord could have been cleared; but no, it was just another part of the great whitewash; the outrageous conspiracy to destroy him.'

Leslie Harrison puts it rather differently:

"The first public reference to Naess's 'report' appears to have been on 9 June, 1928, in a newspaper interview. Its apparent 'concealment' was simply that its possible significance was in no way appreciated by Naess and anyone else who knew of his 'report' until Kjell A. Wig, a Norwegian TV producer, picked it up and used it as a basis for a feature in April, 1962 on the 50th Anniversary of the Titanic disaster.

Claes-Göran Wetterholm also comments: 'As far as I know, the Naess statement was not forwarded to the public until 1962, shortly before Naess's death. The statement was first published by the Norwegian Broadcasting Corporation (Norsk Ringkring-Kastning), but I have never heard that the Norwegian government was informed at all about the incident.'

But he agrees with me absolutely about the integrity of Captain Lord. 'I am fully convinced he was used as a scapegoat to cover the mistakes of the Board of Trade. It is tragic that nothing can yet be done to re-open the case, as it becomes more and more obvious that Stanley Lord was innocent' he concludes.

Figure 15.
Claes-Göran Wetterholm, with his own book on the Titanic.
The first to be published in Swedish since 1912.

(Picture by Maria Djurskog)

HANDS OFF THE TITANIC

CHAPTER FIVE:

No 'Royals' on board

Chapter Five: No 'Royals' On Board

There were no Royal personnages on board the Titanic, though many of their friends were among the passengers on that never-to-be-forgotten maiden voyage.

On April 16, 1912, White Star officials at Liverpool received telegrams of sympathy from the King and Queen and the Queen Mother. The King's telegram, sent from Sandringham to the managing director of the company, said:

'The Queen and I are horrified at the appalling disaster which has happened to the Titanic and at the terrible loss of life. We deeply sympathise with the bereaved relatives and feel for them in their great sorrow with all our hearts.'

Figure 16

In reply to the King's message, the firm sent the following telegram: 'We are deeply grateful to your Majesty and the Queen for the gracious message of sympathy. This calamity is indeed overwhelming in its magnitude and in the sorrow it must bring to so many hearts. We are taking necessary steps to secure that the news of your Majesties' sympathy shall reach all those for whom it is intended.'

George V., 1865-1936 (R. 1910-1936), was King of England and Emperor of India, which sub-continent he had visited for the Coronation Durbar just four months before the Titanic's sailing.

There is much compassion in that signature... authority, too. The long run-in to his name shows the importance the King attached to tradition. Paternalistic, father of six, he was very much the family man, yet at the same time, had a genuine feeling for all his people. The tone of that telegram proves the depth of his grief for the victims of the Titanic disaster. The signature confirms his sincerity.

It is fortunate that the First Lord of the Admiralty did not take it into his head to set off on that maiden voyage either. Had he done so and been lost, as he well might have been, the whole course of history would have been changed. Because the man who held that post at the time was none other than Mr. (later Sir) Winston Churchill. (1874-1965).

Figure 17   *Yours sincerely*
                Winston S. Churchill

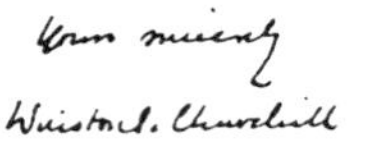

This very small writing is reminiscent of Einstein's. Such a tiny script often comes from writers with great analytical or scientific skills.

At the time of the Titanic disaster, the British Prime Minister was Herbert Henry Asquith, First Earl of Oxford (1852-1928; who held office, 1910-1918).

Here, for the record, is his signature:

Figure 18   *H H Asquith*

It is an upright, yet quirky little hand: scholarly, but not at all in the traditional mould. The reverse turn of the 'q', like that of Churchill's 'y', suggest altruism. Indeed, Asquith upheld the concept of old age pensions, suffragettes, Welsh disestablishment and Irish Home Rule. The way that final stroke of the 'h' drops, un-necessarily, into the lower zone shows a very awkward streak in his nature.

Figure 19   *William H. Taft*

William H. Taft, 27th President of the United States of America (1857-1930; who held office, 1909-1913) was not on board, either. But at least two of his close personal friends were and both were lost. One, Major Archibald Butt, was his aide-de-camp; the other, William T. Stead, writer and psychic investigator, was going to New York at the President's invitation, to address a peace conference at Carnegie Hall on April 21.

On hearing of the tragedy, the President sent a personal message to the King, expressing condolences of the American people to their 'kinsmen across the sea'.

Asquith and Taft were both lawyers, by profession: a couple of quick-thinkers. Judging them on their signatures alone; of the two, the Prime Minister appears to have been the more intellectual, the President the more intuitive.

The phenomenon of two different people having a similar style of writing was briefly referred to and explained in the previous chapter.

Earlier in this chapter, the signature of King George V was reproduced.

Here it is again, now followed by that of his son, George VI, who acceeded some years later on the abdication of his uncrowned brother, Edward VIII.

As we shall see, the son is heavily influenced by the father.

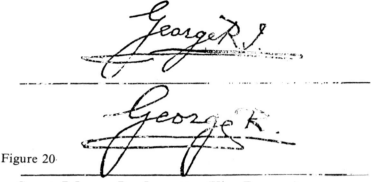

Figure 20

George R.I., was Rex Imperator (King Emperor).

What a wild and excitable character he was. It is strange how signs of one's interests and hobbies or professions sometimes show up in the signature.

This is no ordinary underlining. Examine it closely and you will see how it could be taken to resemble a shotgun and of course, this King was very much a hunting and shooting man.

What a temper he had. Note the heavy start of the R., with its thick blob. His social prejudices are also manifest. See the high-handed execution of the G. He was very much· a man for standing on ceremony . . . and a far more dominant ruler than his son, the reluctant monarch.

By the time George VI came to the throne, the British Empire had dissolved, hence the dropping of the letter I.

George VI was an intensely shy man, with a stammer and a nature so hesitant that were it not for the support and downright common sense of his wife (the present Queen Mother), he would probably never have been able to face up to his unexpected responsibilities. He did, however, rise to the position and his compassion for his people during the troubled years of the Second World War made him one of the most popular rulers ever.

It would seem from his handwriting that George VI turned for inspiration to the memory of his father. The paternal influence is very strong. Note the same rightward slant, the similarly formed structure of the letters and the heavy double underlining.

But now, look closer.

Appearances can be very deceptive. The rightward slant is natural enough in a man who believes he ought to mix with his people (which he certainly did during those war years). His father was a good mixer too, only in his case it was mainly with the shooting fraternity.

The similarly-formed letter structures are simply a mark of his upbringing, traditions, social mores and the like.

And the underlining? Although at first glance it appears to resemble that on the signature above it, on closer inspection it turns out to be entirely different.

Pick up a pen and outline each as they were written. George V lifts his pen and writes his underscore as a separate entity. He starts his beneath the first 'e' of his name, runs the line to the right, doubles back on it, then produces a final stroke back in to end almost where he started.

George VI does not lift his pen at this point. He zooms on down at an angle, then changes direction to follow a similar course to that of his father, then back he comes again, only here he continues to the right in what might have developed into a real downward curve had it progressed much further. Almost as if he felt he should have been more 'sporty', but couldn't really work up the enthusiasm.

Another significant difference is the way each king has written that very important letter 'R' (rex).

George V has attached it to his name, as if it were an integral part of his being. As a man born to be king, it is his identity.

For George VI it appears almost as an afterthought. He expected to be no more exalted than Duke of York; the 'kingship' as we all know, was thrust upon him and his signature shows exactly how he felt about that.

His is an altogether nicer hand than that of his father . . . more compassionate, more kind, more thoughtful. Not the teeniest trace of temper.

And, if all this begs the question 'what on earth have the kings of England to do with the sinking of Titanic'; the honest answer has to be 'nothing at all'.

They are here only to show how, when one person is influenced by another, it can show up in the handwriting.

Captain Stanley Lord needs no introduction at this stage. The signature reproduced with his, is that of his son.

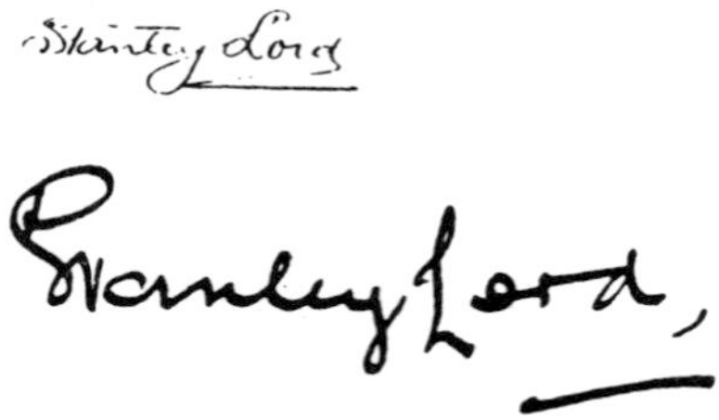

Stanley Lord

Figure 21 _Stanley Lord,_

The captain's writing has been reduced in size and has grown a little faint with the years; both of which factors make the signature of his son seem much larger and heavier, which in reality it is not.

Strong similarities show themselves here, too. Both are upright and stylish: the signatures of gentlemen; showing kindness, thoughtfulness and reflecting a belief in high standards.

Both reflect the dignity and high morals of each writer. They contain similar letter formations and are, again, both underlined.

There is nothing vague or indeterminate about either signature. Both men are seen to be steady and dependable. Captain Lord and his son would always put the interests of others before themselves.

The main difference, as I see it, is in the structure of the capitals. The captain's capitals are in perfect proportion to the lower-case letters, whereas those of his son are larger and much more dominant. They are, as it were, making a statement.

These large capitals would suggest that Stanley Lord, the second, is accustomed to making himself perfectly clear. He is concise and articulate.

His father's signature is more in the nature of 'take me as you find me'; the son's, with those capitals, shows the importance he attaches to making himself understood.

Neither is that of a man who would allow himself to be browbeaten, but that of the son does indicate his ability to spell out the facts and expect justice in return.

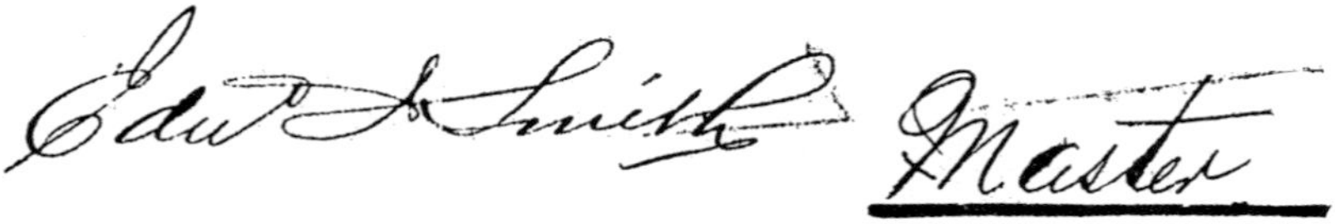

Edwd J Smith   Master

Figure 22 _Don Smith_

Here we have Captain Smith (analysed in Chapter One) signing himself in full, rather than simply E.J., as already featured and his great-nephew Mr. Donald Smith abbreviating his own name to Don.

The captain, as already pointed out, was an outgoing type and so proud of his role of master of the ship which was to be his last before retiring. It is a most positive and forthright hand.

The signature beneath it is also positive and proud. Note the size of that capital S: showing the importance attached to the family name. Note too, the backward swing of the capital D, revealing an absorbing interest in tradition and family background.

It is an intuitive hand; highly individualistic.

Captain Edward John Smith was a great one for social mixing: Mr. Donald Smith would appear to be less extravert, though there is evidence of a dry sense of humour.

The abrupt ending of the final 'h' shows that he is not one for lingering over anything, unnecessarily. This style of writing reveals the nature of someone who is liable to end a conversation if people begin to bore him; and in that respect he would seem to differ from his great uncle, who would be far more likely to have put up with bores (and the dismal conversation of dreary passengers) in the name of duty.

HANDS OFF THE TITANIC

CHAPTER SIX:
Originators

Chapter Six: Originators

The White Star liner, Titanic was the second of three sister ships built by Messrs. Harland and Wolff Ltd., at Queen's Island, Belfast. The others were Olympic (1911-1935) and Britannic (1914-1916), the name of which was originally to have been Gigantic, but was changed after the Titanic disaster.

All three were intended to be bigger and better than any other vessels afloat: Harland and Wolff excelled themselves in the building of these three magnificent liners for the White Star Line.

'Titanic was scheduled to sail from Belfast on 1st April, 1912, but owing to a strong north-westerly wind, her departure was postponed until the following day.' explains Michael McCaughan.

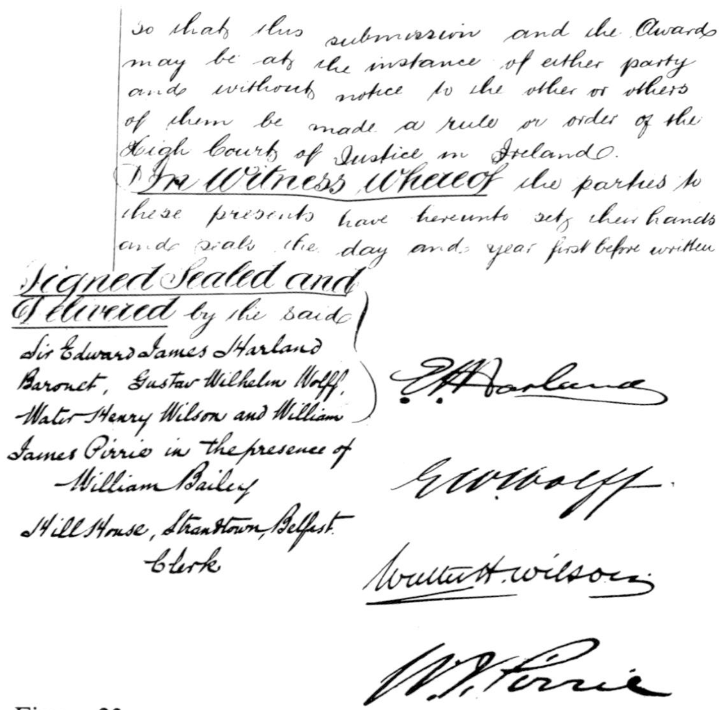

so that this submission and the Awards may be at the instance of either party and without notice to the other or others of them be made a rule or order of the High Court of Justice in Ireland.

In Witness Whereof the parties to these presents have hereunto set their hands and seals the day and year first before written

Signed Sealed and Delivered by the said Sir Edward James Harland Baronet, Gustav Wilhelm Wolff, Walter Henry Wilson and William James Pirrie in the presence of William Bailey Hill House, Strandtown, Belfast. Clerk

E J Harland

G W Wolff

Walter H. Wilson

W J Pirrie

Figure 23

'It is safe to predict that the Olympic and Titanic will enhance the great reputation already enjoyed by the Line: they are without peer on the ocean: though so large, they are beautiful, alike in their appearance and in the simplicity of the working arrangements. Everything on board has been well — in many cases, brilliantly — conceived and admirably carried out.' announced a contemporary White Star publicity booklet, reproduced in McCaughan's book.

Nobody would argue about the beauty of these vessels, and the dedicated work which went into designing and building them. So let us flash back a further twenty seven years, to see what can be gleaned from the minds of the originators. To Messrs. Harland and Wolff plc, I am indebted for the specimen signatures of the four partners of the company, reproduced from a document signed on 18 December, 1885.*9

Sir Edward Harland (1831 — 1895)
What an unusual looking E.

Sir Edward must have been quite a man. Yes, yes, we know that the letter was intended to look something like ⟨✍⟩ but instead, ended up as ⟨✍⟩ which is just the teeniest bit quirky, don't you think?

Sir Edward clearly enjoyed breaking with convention. He seems to have had the ability to enter a room and cause quite a stir because of his eccentricity: to hold them momentarily in awe (when writing the J, he is still being unorthodox!) then, just when they had accepted his offbeat presentation, he would surprise them further by switching back to tradition and becoming thoroughly conventional.

Rock solid, this man and cute as a fox. The angle inside the loop of that E reveals a very calculating mind.

He was always one step ahead of his competitors: indeed, he may not even have acepted that he HAD any competitors. This was a clever man: very clever indeed. Perceptive, alert to everything going on around him.

He appears to have had a nice sense of humour too (the curves of the E, the 'smile-shaped' letter connections . . . and how about those little dots beneath the E and the J?). Most people who combine full stops with underlining do only one and place it to the right of the signature. But then, Sir Edward Harland was hardly 'most people'. The only other case of a double dot after an underlining is that of Richard Garrett, the author, whose signature is analysed in Chapter 12.

Gustav Wilhelm Wolff (1834 — 1913)
Born in Hamburg, he studied engineering in Liverpool and Manchester, was MP for East Belfast from 1892.

Here was the perfect foil for Sir Edward; conventional, consistent and inclined to be artistic. This writing is sharp and shaded (upward strokes executed lightly, and the downward heavily), pointing to a sharp and critical mind.

The inhibited upper loops of the 'l' and double 'f' suggest that his personal relationships with the opposite sex might not have been too satisfactory, but Herr Wolff's mind dwelt only lightly on such matters. His future lay in business and he was determined to keep it that way.

Note how unwilling he is to let go the pen. See how it runs on, way ahead, until it actually merges with the seal.

Walter Henry Wilson (1839 — 1904)

This gentleman was very much in the shadow of Sir Edward: though deep down he must have known there was no comparison. Like the great man, he too starts his signature with a big, high rising letter, but he soon falls short. The style, the flamboyance, the magnetism are simply not there.

Nor can he even keep his end up long enough to impress anyone. By the time he reaches the second W it is almost as small as his lower case letters. The underscore is a poor imitation of the senior partner's. He starts off like his chief but, once more, gives up trying and launches into the sharp, angular shape which is quite individualistic.

This shows an odd mixture of aggression and eroticism.

William J. Pirrie (1847 — 1924)

This signature is big and bold and scratchy: pasty — or 'pastose' as some graphologists might term it. A sensuous man; hot-headed, hot-blooded, with a positively freaky sense of humour (how many people would dot the 'i' INSIDE the loop of the P?)

In his own way, the man who was later to become Lord Pirrie, was as dominant and awkward a character as Sir Edward.

Just as Sir Edward tended to break with convention when writing his first letter, so did William J. Pirrie.

Conventional formation of the letter is P (stem first; top to bottom; then loop, in a clockwise movement).

Here we have $\mathcal{P}$ (loop first, anti-clockwise, running straight into the stem in a single movement).

In their own way, therefore, these four men were all different, but they complemented each other well enough . . . with perhaps one possible exception.

66

Wilson, somehow, did not appear to possess quite the same panache and dynamism of the other three.

Pirrie joined the firm of Harland and Wolff at the age of fifteen as an apprentice draughtsman and worked his way right to the top of the company until, at the time of Titanic's launch, he was chairman and managing director of the company. This second sample of his signature was penned shortly after the disaster.

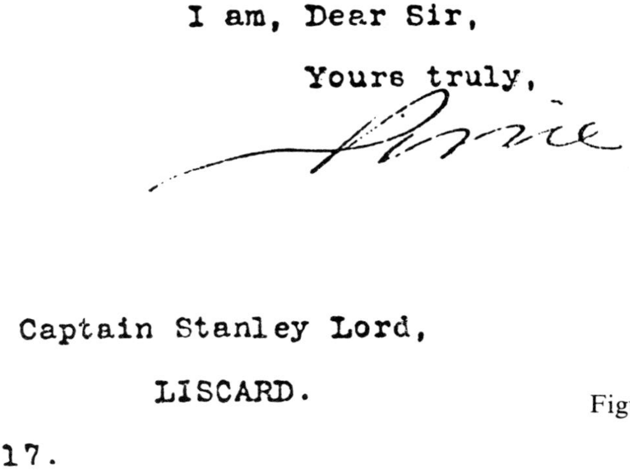

I am, Dear Sir,

Yours truly,

Captain Stanley Lord,

LISCARD.

Figure 24

17.

Gone now is humorous placing of the i dot inside the upper loop of the capital. Instead, it has moved over to its correct position above the i and has been made in a downward movement, rather than upward, as before; reflecting his depression.

Gone, too, is the pastose script. This pressure is very much weaker; but then, at this stage, so was the writer's health.

The basic shape of the capital P is still essentially the same only now it swings back dramatically to the left, in a very definite glance to the past. And again that downward stroke.

He had, after all, not just lost his beautiful ship, but also Thomas Andrews, his beloved nephew and personal assistant, who had taken his place on the voyage, because Pirrie himself was about to have a prostate operation.

Certainly, his poor state of health is very noticeable; particularly in the pressure changes of his writing. The physiological weakness is most apparent in the capital P, where it can be seen in a sort of dotted line and elsewhere, in the many broken connecting strokes (note too, the fractured, finale).

Lord Pirrie was not at all well when he penned this note and his failing health appeared to have affected his temperament. The signs seem to point to a cantankerous old man.

That enlarged and arrogant final 'e' suggests he had grown accustomed to putting people down (particularly those he considered less well placed than himself).

The signature is well placed and so is the writer. If we take the swinging leftward stroke into account, we see that one short name measuring almost half the width of the page.

Lord Pirrie, one might safely assume, zealously guarded his position. After all, he had worked extremely hard to reach it.

Figure 25   *Thomas Andrews*

When the Titanic trials began on April 2, 1912, from Belfast to the Isle of Man, the thirty nine year old Thomas Andrews was on board and very enjoyable he found it all too.

His conclusion about the trials: 'very satisfactory'.

How sad he did not survive to make a similar observation about the maiden voyage of the ship that he helped his uncle to build.

When I visited the Titanic Exhibition mounted at the Ulster Folk and Transport Museum (on the outskirts of Belfast) to mark the 75th Anniversary of the sinking, I was able to examine one of the most poignant mementoes of Thomas Andrews. It was his box of drawing instruments, still in their original wooden, velvet-lined case: the selfsame instruments with which, presumably, he contributed to the design of the new liner.

Thomas Andrews was a friend of Bruce Ismay.

Like his uncle, he too entered the ship-builders as an apprentice . . . in his case, at sixteen. He too made his way up the scale, eventually qualifying as an architect and engineer.

When the ship foundered, Andrews emerged as one of the heroes of the night . . . telling passengers to put on their coats and prepare to leave. He helped many of them into lifeboats. When last seen, he was busy throwing chairs and other objects to people struggling in the water . . . advising them to cling on to anything they could reach. Never, for one moment, did he give a thought to his own safety.

He left a widow, Nellie and a baby daughter, Elizabeth.

The signature of Thomas Andrews shows him to have been a much more pleasant man than his uncle; more down to earth too, as indicated by the very unassuming capital A, which is really only an

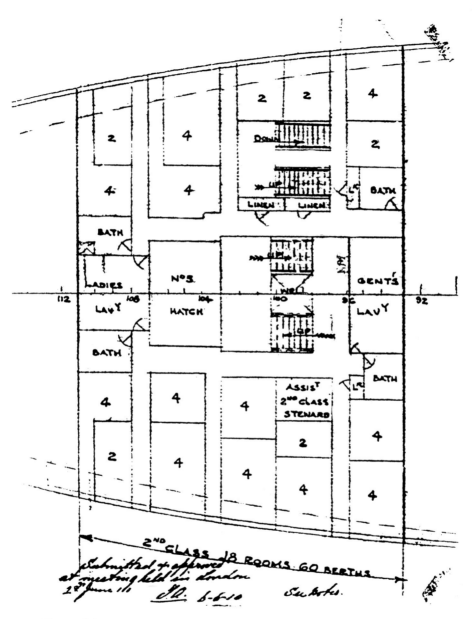

Figure 26

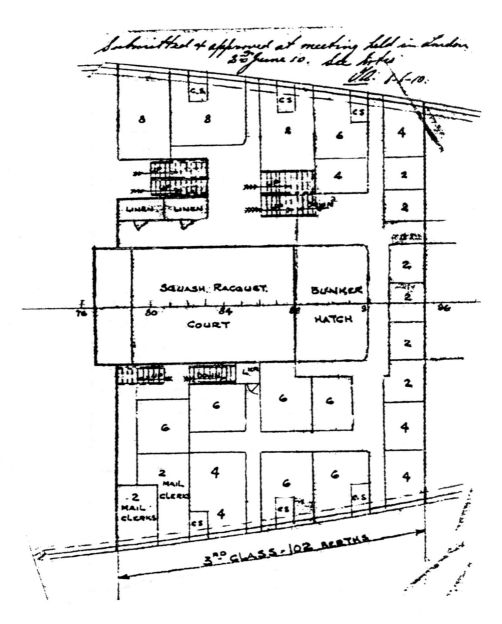

Figure 27

enlarged version of the lower case form. This was not a man to stand on ceremony, or to expect caps to be doffed at him.

The 's' at the end of Thomas is 'submissive' (written thus: *ɔʃ*) whereas that at the end of Andrews is 'dominanat' (*S*); which shows he had a rare ability to be either, or both, on demand.

He was clever, strong, enthusiastic: a pleasure to be with.

Even in this very limited sample, a most attractive fusion in style and movement is evident. There is not a single flaw in this hand... it is most consistent, showing the writer to be calm, brave, hardworking: a thoroughly decent type.

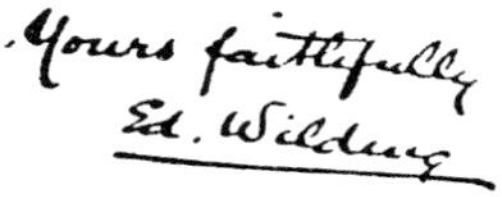

Figure 28 *Yours faithfully Ed. Wilding*

Edward Wilding was a naval architect; one of the design team responsible for the construction of Titanic.

His is a small, neat and very artistic hand. It is constant, lyrical and fast moving, despite its virtual lack of slant. The high flying 'i' dot and long running 't' bar show Wilding's thoughts to have regularly run ahead of his pen. This signature is delightfully free of ornamentation. It is the straightforward hand of a man who does not believe in wasting time or energy. It is, admittedly, somewhat reserved and inhibited.

Nevertheless, this man knew what he was about. He was a first rate craftsman who, although one of a team, seemed happier working alone.

The drooping signature hints at depression. The underscoring stresses belief in himself and his abilities. This sample, written just a few months after the sinking, appears to contain an element of guilt. He appears to have been blaming himself for something over which he had no control; and how many of us can say we have never done that?

Edward Wilding was a perfectionist.

His creation was perfect.

The fact that it sank could hardly be blamed on him . . . .

Now here was a self-opinionated character. A fussy type, who appeared to pay more attention to secondary issues than important ones (note the little affectations — the extra, ornamental, strokes on the 's'; the imperious 'y', the unusual underscore).

The signature is much larger and more dominant (domineering?) than the other words.

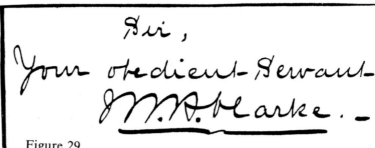

Figure 29

Compare the size of the 's' in 'Sir' with the 'M' in his own name — denoting how much more he thought of himself than of 'Sir' — whoever he might be. This is not a man with whom I should like to argue.

Conceited and arrogant, he would always pull rank on lesser mortals and have the last word in an argument (full stop after the name, combined with underscore).

Maurice Harvey Clarke made a point of being different from (superior to?) the multitudes.

So who was this Mr. Clarke with all the undesirable traits?

He was immigration officer for the Board of Trade. His function was to clear Titanic under the Merchant shipping Acts as an immigrant ship . . . in other words, to give official clearance for Titanic to sail.

*⁹Having duly conducted my analyses on the founders of Harland and Wolff, I wrote to the company, asking for comment and received from their spokesman the following reply: 'Walter Wilson was one of the first gfentlemen apprentices taken into the Yard in 1857 and, as a boy, was apparently interested in making model engines from scrap metal. In 1868, he was appointed Yard manager and in 1875, on the dissolution of the old partnership between Edward Harland and Gustav Wolff, was taken into the partnership. Wilson was regarded as hard working but shy. He was a practical Naval Architect more at home with technical rather than financial matters. He retired in 1901 to grow orchids.'

HANDS OFF THE TITANIC

CHAPTER SEVEN:
Officers and Crew

Chapter Seven: Officers and Crew

Much has already been written about Second Officer Lightoller.

In 1912, lifeboat drill was not compulsory and it had not taken place on the Titanic, but Lightoller's confidence that the great ship would not, or could not, sink conveyed itself to others. In the immediate aftermath of the brush with the iceberg, therefore, there was no panic. It was a bitterly cold night and passengers were in no great rush to leave the safety of the decks where they were assembled and go off into the tiny boats. The drop of seventy feet did not look too appealing, but the main cause of apprehension was the idea of being adrift in a boat for what might turn out to be a rather long time. It was cold enough on deck; they knew it would be colder still once they hit the water. Many declared they would stay aboard . . . at least until the situation became clearer. . . .

The boats had all gone.

Lightoller was one of the last survivors to jump from the sinking ship. Suction pulled him and held him against a grating, from which he tried repeatedly to free himself. Just as he was about to give up, a blast of hot air blew him free and pushed him in the direction of a capsized Engelhardt 'collapsible' lifeboat, onto which he clambered. Despite the fact that he was soaking wet and dressed in nothing more substantial than trousers and pullover, he automatically took control of the situation, showing others on the raft with him how to keep afloat throughout that long, dark night. All told, there were about thirty aboard the collapsible.

Lightoller was the last Titanic survivor to be picked up by the Carpathia.

Figure 30

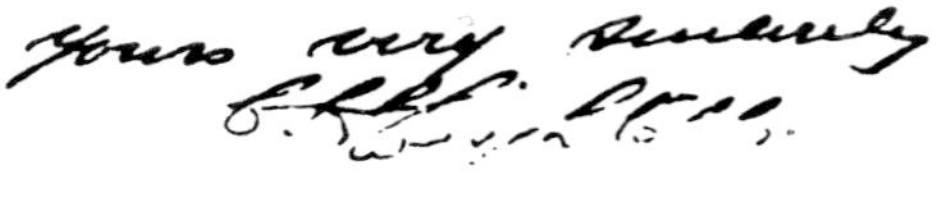

So what does his handwriting tell us about him?

Unfortunately, there is very little to go on, but it does show a lovely consistency, with its speedy and regular flow. The writing is that of a real man of action. He would appear to have had tremendous energy and vivacity. On the face of it, he appears to be refreshingly clear of any complexities of character.

Lightoller had a sharp, alert mind. He was a man who liked to stick to his guns. Apart from the demands of those closest to him he was not a man to become emotionally entangled at a personal level (the clue is in the under-developed under-zones, and the inhibited loops in the upper zone, particularly on the l's).

He could occasionally tie himself up in knots (which is natural I suppose for a sailor, but I'm thinking metaphorically ... the clue this time being in the looped and knotted f's); but he could wriggle out of them just as easily. One gets the impression that if he liked someone, he would say so. If he did not like them he was also likely to say so. This was not a man to become involved in back-biting or tittle-tattle. Just one little sign bothers me about this hand. No, 'bother' is not exactly true. It intrigues me.

Certain variations in pressure point to a health problem.

The changes seen here, though, are quite different to those noticed in the signature of Lord Pirrie. Pirrie's bodily weakness was generalised; the failing health and stamina of an elderly man (although being only 65 at the time of signing that particular letter, he should not yet have been showing such signs).

What we have here, is much more specific, because it takes the form of quite clear breaks in the letter formations.

To use an analogy: it is the difference between a snail dragging itself wearily along, leaving its shiny trail for all to see, and a show jumper leaping over fences; the hoof marks being strong and clear everywhere, except where the actual jumps have taken place.

Not for one moment am I comparing His Lordship to a snail and the Second Officer to a horse; I am attempting by the use of metaphor, to illustrate the way the pen moves on paper. In one, it is weak, but generalised; in the other, it is strong apart from where those spasmodic changes occur.

In most cases like the second one mentioned above, there is a clinical explanation. A minor irregularity of heartbeat, such as with an extra systolic murmer, will register in the brain and, working its way down the neural pathways and motor mechanisms of the arm, will cause the hand to jump for a split second. This, then, will leave the teeniest little break in many of the upper loops: often visible only under strong magnification.

This phenomenon can usually be traced back to be a complication of rheumatic, or scarlet, fever in childhood.

I stress the word 'usually' (of which more, anon.).

First, though can anyone say whether the Titanic's Second Officer did, in fact, have a childish bout of either illness? And do we know if he was prone to suffer from fatigue on exertion, minor attacks of breathlessness and perhaps even some discomfort in the region of his heart?

The signs in this sample would seem to suggest that the writer's heart was slightly deficient; though, at that point, not enough to have proved any immediate danger to life. It would have been operating merely in a state of impaired efficiency.

Lesser mortals than Lightoller might find it necessary to restrict the amount of exertion undertaken, in the belief that if any strain were thrown on such a heart, it might yield.

But the whole tone of this man's writing shows that he was not one to pander to any personal weakness; even if it were potentially serious. At the time of the Titanic disaster, the last person he would be likely to consider would have been himself.

If Lightoller's heart were, indeed, slightly deficient, then to have survived the horrors of that April night, he must have been an even more remarkable man than any have given him credit for . . . though my gut reaction on seeing these quirky little signs is that surely the events of that night must have taken their toll on him in later life . . . whether the cause was childhood fever, or not.

As intimated, above, there is an alternative explanation for Lightoller's irregularity of heartbeat.

Lengthy immersion in the water may not have exaccerbated the problem, but instead, actually caused it. Whereas in most cases where these very specific changes of pressure are manifest, the explanation is childhood fever, here because of the very unusual circumstances, we may have something quite different.

Lightoller dived into the sea from the top of the wheelhouse and clambered out of the water on to the collapsible as soon as he could. His immersion in the ice cold water may not have been for very long, but sometimes on these occasions, five minutes can seem like five hours and naturally, his blood temperature would have fallen; dropping rapidly from its normal level of 82.4 degrees Fahrenheit to many degrees lower. This sort of situation can cause the victim to suffer in a variety of ways; he can become dozey, perhaps even lose consciousness. It is not unknown for the heart to begin to palpitate and show signs of abnormality.

When I originally made the above observations, I had not seen a sample of writing produced by Lightoller before his night in the water, so at that stage had no way of saying for certain whether the irregularity of heartbeat was present before the tragedy or was caused by it. Without such a sample, I couild not definitively establish the cause of the missed beats.

But I was then presented with an autograph written on the very day Titanic set off on her maiden voyage. There, clear as a bell are those selfsame tell-tale signs.

Figure 31

So now, I can say for sure that the problem was not caused by immersion in cold water; though that particular experience would not have done him much good.

If he DID have a minor problem with his heart, as the evidence does now appear to suggest, then the signs are that it WOULD have yielded eventually. Yet how sensibly this remarkable man mush have lived, for he survived to the age of seventy eight; the last surviving senior officer of the Titanic (though he was actually outlived by two officers junior to him — Pitman, Third and Boxhall, Fourth) . . . .

And there my observations about the Second Officer ground to a halt until I was fortunate enough to encounter Patrick Stenson, Lightoller's biographer.

Having read my conclusions about the subject of his book, he observed:

"I found the suggestion that he had a heart defect dating back to before the Titanic intriguing. He did actually die of heart problems, not helped by the effects of the London fog of 1952/3 and the fact that he liked his cigarettes.

"However, the only possible cause I can offer as to heart abnormality in Lightoller's prime years was the heavy bout of malaria he contracted down the West African Coast in the 1890's, which had a habit of returning for several years afterwards, until it apparently disappeared at the turn of the century (when he was aged twenty five). Could this have caused some 'pin prick' defect in the heart mechanism, do you think?"

Frankly I did not know. Malaria is caused by a single-cell parasite, which is transmitted by the bite of an anopholes mosquito; but I was unsure about how its pathogenic effects might relate to the handwriting. Malaria certainly causes fever and the parasitic presence in the bloodstream can also result in anaemia. But could either be responsible for what we have here? Never having encountered this particular phenomenon before, I invited the opinion of a clinical expert at the Liverpool School of Tropial Medicine. "There are several species of malaria parasite" he explained. "Some HAVE been known to enter the internal organs: most commonly the brain and kidney, but a few of the rarer species have been known to affect the heart." But can we totally exclude the possibility of malaria as the original cause of this man's problem, I wondered. "No" concluded the expert "We cannot" . . . .

Figure 32

Fourth Officer Joseph Boxhall also survived and here are two samples of his writing, one penned in 1912, the other produced many years later, when he was a very elderly gentleman. Young or old, his is a most imperious and dominant style. J. Groves Boxhall, he signs himself in his twenties. Fifty-one years later, he has become Commander Joseph Groves Boxhall . . . still imperious, still dominant. His is a hand of enormous strength and energy, very powerful and positive. The type to command respect from anyone: even his peers.

With a signature like that, no doubt his fellow officers on the Titanic would have jumped to attention at the very sight of him; just as his chums probably did in childhood. He may well have been a 'Bossy Boots' at school. But there was no harm in this man.

The general impression to come from this hand in old age is that of a man who liked to spread himself out all over the place; just as the words on his letter have done on the paper. Tidiness was not exactly Boxhall's middle name . . . at least, not in his advancing years.

Here, though, was a man with great powers of perception and intuition (angular-shaped i dots; disjointed writing); a dogmatic type, prone to eccentricity. A character.

How proud he was to have been associated with the Titanic. Note how he has subconsciously turned several of his small t's into mini-capitals . . . 'assist' (second line from bottom); 'just', 'at', 'moment' (all on the bottom line).

Some of the letters are beginning to fracture as the pressure itself weakens towards the end, but then, as he points out in the footnote of his letter: 'You must realise that I am an old man, close on seventy nine'. But what a man he was in his day.

That writing shows him to have been quite unique. Wonderful company — a man who would either hold you enthralled, or bore you to tears, depending on circumstances. The sort of man you would either loathe on sight, or love for the rest of your life.

In death, as in life, Boxhall remained highly individual. When he died in April, 1967, the ashes of Titanic's Fourth Officer were stewn over what was then believed to have been the site of her sinking (though was subsequently found to have been somewhat off course). Nevertheless, Boxhall achieved his final ambition: to be back with his Captain and fellow officers . . . .

And now, to Chief Purser Herbert McElroy: first, for a pre-sailing signature.

Figure 33

78

11 Walcott Avenue
Laurie

Jany 3rd/63. Christchurch Hants.

Dear Sir — The "Times" Cutting
of your advertisement requiring
official minutes concerning
"Titanic" enquiries has been
sent to me by my Niece in
Norwich. I was H° Officer of
the Ship and rem'd [...] the
last of the 4 Surviving Officers.
I should like to be able
to assist you but unfortunately
Just at the moment I cannot —

from "A Night to Remember" one
Mr Wm. M°Quitty who intended
presenting them to a museum in
Belfast — afterwards regretted it
I don't know where you reside
but after the train from Hexle
him — Stanley Williamson — Features
Producer. Made Report. Similar
endeavour to show you what
share in my possession.
Yours Sincerely
Joseph Foster Bottrell.
Commander RNR Ret'd.

from "A Night to Remember"
page 179.

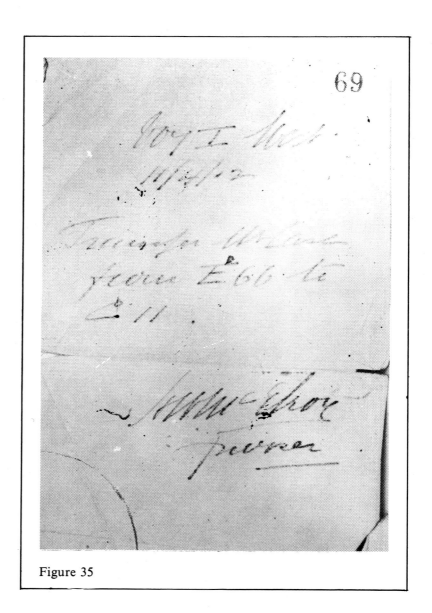

Figure 35

His pencilled note to Steward William Faulkner, referred to in Chapter Three, is reproduced hereunder. The purser, like so many members of Titanic's crew, helped load passengers into the boats, but made no attempt to board one himself. When the order came from Captain Smith for each man to fend for himself, Herbert McElroy shook hand with fellow officer, Charles Lightoller and said goodbye. He was never seen again.

The garland style of this writing shows the purser's love of luxury. Like so many others featured in these pages, he too underlined his signature and his designation: showing how important he considered his work to be and how much he enjoyed it.

McElroy was a man of style and panache. Note the lovely capital I. He was probably better known by his Christian name than his surname, because the first capital rises way above the second. There is a strong sense of conformity here.

The long run in to some of the letters reflects his sense of pride in family and tradition.

He was also a good social mixer; a man with his priorities in the right place. A thoroughly good type.

The 69, by the way, is the number of the page he tore out of his notebook . . . .

Fleet was stationed in the crow's nest when, at 11.40 p.m., on the night in question, he first sighted and passed on the information about The Iceberg. He rang the warning bell, 'phoned the bridge and called out 'Iceberg right ahead'.

Then he remained in position until relieved at midnight and an hour or so later, finally left the sinking ship in a lifeboat.

Fred Fleet did his duty and had nothing for which to reprimand himself. Yet it was subsequently claimed that had Fleet and G.A. Hogg, the lookout who took over from him, been provided with binoculars, they would have seen the iceberg much earlier and could have averted the collision.

Responding to the claim, Lightoller told the British Inquiry (held on 21st May, 1912):

"I would only give glasses to men I could thoroughly trust, but if a man did not report until after he had used his glasses, then I utterly condemn glasses."

The findings of this inquiry:

"The use of binoculars by the lookout men was not necessary or usual in the circumstances."

Many years later, in 1956, a doctor claimed that the reason why Titanic struck ice was because the lookout had 'night blindness'.

This, he stressed, was not due to inattention or sleeping on watch. Night blindness, explained the doctor, made it difficult for people to distinguish objects and could prevent them from seeing anything at all beyond a certain distance. Fleet, like the rest of the crew, was probably lacking in Vitamin A, which caused the condition.

Leslie Harrison absolutely dismisses the night blindness theory and explained to me his reasons for doing so:

"Recalling my personal experience of very many hours of watchkeeping in complete darkness during the war, I cannot believe that Fleet could hold down such an intensively competitive (and selective) job as lookout in a valuable passenger liner if his eyesight differed even marginally from the average. In any event, he sighted an unlit (!) iceberg at three-quarters of a mile range in the dark, which is good enough for me."

Fleet remained in position until relieved at midnight and an hour or so later, finally left the sinking ship in a lifeboat.

Reproduced here are a couple of samples of his autograph: the first having been produced in 1912, the second about half a century later.

Figure 36

Figure 37

The earlier signature has a happy, carefree swing to it. It is consistent in spacing and letter sizes. The baseline is constant. A free-flowing hand, it is that of a man with hardly a care in the world. (It was written before Titanic set sail).

The later signature is very different; and not just because of the years between. It is no longer consistent. Letter sizes vary enormously, the baseline wavers all over the place and it is anything but carefree. It is pasty, shaky and contains a host of inconsistencies. The varying letter sizes and pressure suggest that the writer's eyesight might (at this stage only) be deficient.

It is abundantly clear that when Frederick Fleet wrote this signature, he was in a state of deep depression. Pen trails (seen most clearly by the naked eye on each of the three capital F's) suggest despondency and physical exhaustion. The heavy pressure denotes his very sensual nature, with rounded letters reinforcing the point about his being an emotional sort of person. The whole tone of this signature denotes desperate unhappiness . . . almost as if the writer were a prisoner to his feelings. Great sorrow emerges from this hand.

I shall not dwell on it too much, but would conclude simply that the man who penned it was in urgent need of help at the time of writing: or, perhaps, therapy is a more accurate word — the sort that only a highly skilled professional could provide. This writing is that of a very, very sad man . . . right on the brink of despair.

I subsequently learned that, shortly after producing this shaky signature, the despondent Fred Fleet hanged himself on a clothes line in his garden.

HANDS OFF THE TITANIC

CHAPTER EIGHT:

More of the same

Chapter Eight: More Of The Same.

A further selection of Titanic's crew is featured in the composite illustration containing eight signatures as follows:- 1. The Surgeons; 2. the Marconi telegraphists; 3. Hichens; 4. the Slade brothers; 5. John Priest; 6. John Coffey; 7. Thomas Prentice and 8. 'T. Hart'.

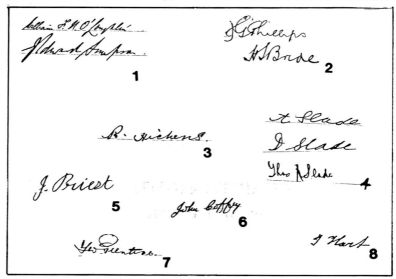

1. Ship's surgeons.
2. Marconi telegraphist: Phillips died, Bride survived.
3. Hichens: the man who was at the wheel at the time of collision.
4. Slade brothers: 'deserters' at Southampton.
5. The hand of a forger.
6. Prentice: Last surviving crewman in England (died, 1982).
7. Coffy: deserted, at Queenstown.
8. Priest: 'Calamity James'? . . . or 'a cat with nine lives'?

1. Titanic's Surgeons: disproving the theory that all doctors write illegibly, the ship's surgeons make themselves perfectly clear. (Perhaps the fact that they were Irishmen had something to do with it . . . old Dr. O'Loughlin hailed from Co. Kerry, while his young assistant, Edward Simpson, came from Belfast). They made a good team, being alike in so many ways: the acute rightward slant of their writing shows each to have been generally outgoing. Small middle

zone, combined with high flying uppers suggest these two men were intellectuals and very much in accord. Yet, despite their friendliness and ability to mix with the crew, these medics both show how rigidly they adhered to the Hippocratic Oath. Note the closely sealed tops to the 'a's' and 'o's'; how many secrets must they have taken to their grave. Sadly, both men were lost.

2. The Marconi telegraphists — Phillips and Bride were a couple of bright young men who, like the doctors, were also in complete accord. Both styles are fast moving (see how, in each case, the initials and surname are all joined up) and full of rhythm. Each signature is very positive, though the pressure of Bride's writing would seem to be stronger than that of Phillips; thus indicating that his physical resources were also better developed . . . which undoubtedly accounts for the fact that Bride was saved, while Phillips was lost.

3. Hichens; Quartermaster — was the man at Titanic's wheel when she collided with the iceberg. Frankly, there is something about this writing which I find disconcerting. It has rather too many negative signs for comfort. It lacks rhythm and 'elasticity'; is not anything like as balanced as the samples contained in 1 and 2 above. Here was a very complex character: self-important, self-indulgent. The giveaway signs: capital R with all its unnecessary curves and swirls; the vulgar swing of the capital Hl, the general discrepancy in letter sizes, the wavering baseline and that final, over-large, arrogant 's', showing a tendency towards insubordination. Did this man really swing the wheel as instructed by the Captain when the iceberg was sited? Or did he choose to carry on straight ahead to what John P. Eaton and Charles Haas so aptly describe in their magnificent book of the same name, as 'Destination Disaster'? I could not help wondering.

However, Leslie Harrison — who very kindly read my analyses on all the crew members — did a spot of knuckle-rapping. Not on Hichens. On me.

"There is no possibility AT ALL of Hichens' failing to carry out an emergency order of this nature; apart from its being his DUTY, there would be a responsibility on both officers of the watch to see that it was obeyed. I NEVER gave an important helm order, even in a lowly tramp steamer, without checking to see that it was being carried out — visually by day, by hand at night — feeling that the helm indicator was moving in the right direction."

So there. I reckon I owe the quartermaster an apology.

4. On a lighter — should that read 'more light-headed'? — note, we meet the Slade brothers. This happy trio, A., D. and Thomas, aged 25, 26 and 27 respectively, decided to wet their whistles before setting sail. They boarded Titanic, dutifully signed on with the other crew members, then repaired to a local hostelry. When, eventually, they emerged into Southampton's broad and cruel daylight, the ship was

already on its way. They did not know it at the time, but the 'demon drink' had saved their lives. One glance at these three signatures suggest that the brothers were already quite inebriated when they signed on. Thomas' scrawl is intriguing.

Not only does the writer show signs of having the shakes, he does not even appear to be focussing properly. What on earth is that apology for a letter in the middle of his first and second name? His brothers appear to have been very close to each other, very alike and great friends, but not quite in the same intellectual category as Thomas who, despite the bleary-eyed scrawl, emerges as a man of intuition. He may well have had bad 'vibes' about the proposed trip and removed himself and his brothers away from danger because of some sort of gut feeling he would, quite probably, have been unable to explain . . . at least in his, then, inebriated state.

5.   John Priest was a fireman: and a character with a gift for surrounding himself by mayhem. Was he born with two left feet, or did he just acquire them as he stumbled through life? Whichever, he did always manage to land on those two feet of his, like the proverbial cat with nine lives.

His background: When Titanic's sister ship Olympic was damaged in collision with HMS Hawke in 1911, John Priest was aboard — and survived. When Titanic struck ice and sank, John Priest was aboard — and survived. He also survived the war losses of Titanic's other sister ship Britannic and two other vessels, Alcantara and Donegal. His luck only ran out in 1935 when, at the relatively young age of 48, he died of pneumonia.

So what sort of qualities did Priest possess to survive five shipwrecks, then die in his bed of an illness which should not have killed a big, hefty sailor, strong enough to battle the waters and all the accompanying trauma, with such alarming regularity?

Now there's the most curious thing of all. Amazingly, nothing particularly startling emerges from this man's signature. His writing is big, round and immature: the simple, ordinary hand of a simple, extra-ordinary man. Just born lucky, I suppose. Or unlucky, depending on your viewpoint.

6.   The reason why John Coffy 'deserted' seems quite basic. A fireman, he could be said to have had a fire in his heart. Coffy sailed as far as Queenstown, then left. No prizes for guessing why, but I'll provide a clue. Remember the song about all the nice girls loving a sailor? Well, that's John Coffy: the man with the oh-so-revealing lower zones.

7.   Thomas Prentice was a young storekeeper who not only survived the collision, but lived on . . . and on . . . the last surviving

crewman in England until he died in 1982, aged 93. Prentice was nobody's fool.

His is the hand of someone with a very determined and dominant personality, who was not without a lively imagination (note the top of the 'p' like an inflated balloon ready for take-off; combined with the very positive capital 't', it tells us that this man was ready for anything). The strong and over-long 't' bar shows his ability to cope with strife in whatever form it presented itself . . . as indeed, he must have done many times during his long, long life. What a shame a later sample of Prentice's writing is not available to determine whether it showed all those lively signs. I bet it did.

8.   The unknown man who signed on as 'T. Hart' might have congratulated himself when he stole the papers of the real T. Hart who, like the Slade brothers, was too drunk to sail. Had the mystery man not run off with that discharge book, he might well have been alive today. Or at least, 'yesterday'. Instead, he died, unmourned, because his true identity has never been discovered.

John P. Eaton tells me that Thomas Hart was listed as dead: 'His mother was making arrangements for a memorial service, when he showed up and told her what had happened.'

It is to her credit that Mrs. Hart did not drop dead with shock herself! (Four nil in favour of drink).

However, without having a genuine Hart signature to make the necessary comparisons, it is not possible to go into any great detail about how a graphologist might set about detecting a forgery. All that can be said about this particular writing is that it has a most uncomfortable feel. It contains much over-writing and many blackened strokes; overt signs of criminality. It is a deceitful and thoroughly untrustworthy hand.

And now for a letter from Africa . . . .

C. J. (Jack) Hurst was a stoker on Titanic. He would not have had time for writing letters on board. The letter reproduced here was written twelve years before the voyage.

Jack Hurst wrote this letter home to his wife Louie when he was serving on the African veldt, having just recovered from a bout of fever which had killed many servicemen of a less strong disposition.

The letter was recently discovered by his grand-daughter Diane Beare, at her parents' home in Southampton. Diane's niece, Lucy Feeney (a colleague of mine on the Liverpool Daily Post and Echo) presented it to me for analysis. The letter runs to four pages, much of which contain personal messages to his wife and five children, two of whom (Michael and Edward) he refers to as the 'dovey boys'. I therefore reproduce only the second page of Gunner Hurst's letter and his closing words of greeting. The extract from his letter reads as follows:-

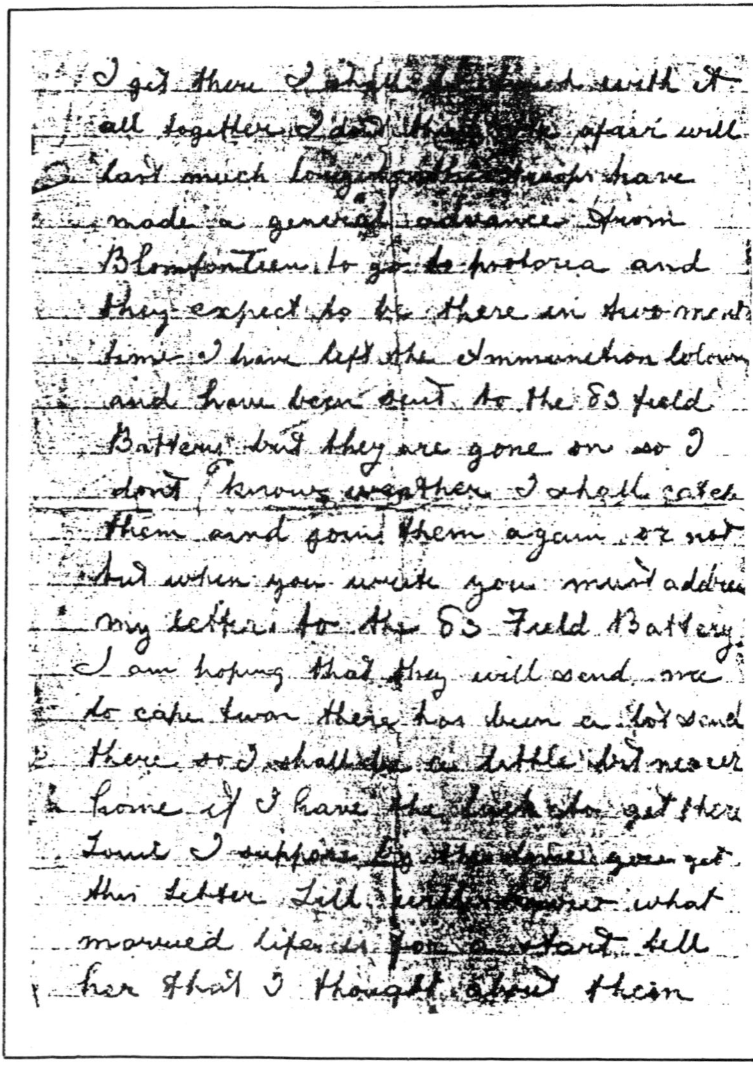
I get there I shall [illegible] with it
all together I don't think the afair will
last much longer [illegible] troops have
made a general advance from
Blomfontein to go to pretoria and
they expect to be there in two month
time I have left the Ammunition Colum
and have been sent to the 83 field
Battery but they are gone on so I
dont know weather I shall catch
them and join them again or not
but when you write you must addres
my letters to the 83 Field Battery
I am hoping that they will send me
to cape town there has been a lot send
there so I shall be a little bit nearer
home if I have the luck to get there
Louie I suppose by the time you get
this letter Lill will know what
married life is for a start tell
her that I thought about them

Figure 39

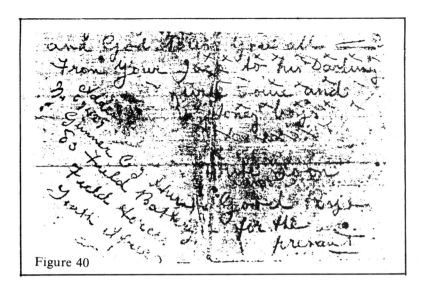

Figure 40

'The troops have made a general advance from Blomfontein to go to Pretoria and they expect to be there in two months' time. I have left the ammunition column and have been sent to the 80 field battery but they are gone on, so I don't know whether I shall catch them and join them again or not, but when you write, you must address my letters to the 80 field battery. I am hoping that they will send me to Capetown . . . .'

and he signs off:-

'So goodbye and God bless you all. From your Jack to his darling wife Louie and his dovey boyś. Write Soon. Goodbye for the present. Address: 69427 Gunner C.J. Hurst, 80 Field Battery, Field . . . South Africa.'

The writing in this letter is pleasant, its weak pressure showing an element of physical weakness (presumably after his recent attack of fever), yet it also reveals basic courage (good, well-formed letter structures) and a lively sense of humour (curved 't' bars, shaped like smiles).

This man was intensely loyal to his wife. The formation of his lower zones indicates that he did not join in the fun and games in which soldiers serving abroad are generally believed to participate.

The vertical writing is almost devoid of slant, showing the writer to have been a proud, upstanding young man. There is hardly a flaw in this character.

How sad that Jack Hurst should have survived the battlefields of Africa, fever and separation from his beloved family, only to have lost his life so prematurely, just twelve years later.

Lucy reflected:

"Being a stoker, he would have been down in the engine rooms at the very bottom of the ship, which is where the water started pouring in immediately she struck ice.

He wouldn't have stood a chance."

Mrs. Hurst's pension from the Titanic fund was one shilling (5p) per child and half a crown (12 ½p) for herself: a total of 37½p per week.

HANDS OFF THE TITANIC

CHAPTER NINE:

First Class passengers

Chapter Nine: First Class Passengers

Time now to take a brief journey into the minds of some of the passengers, to glimpse their various personalities.

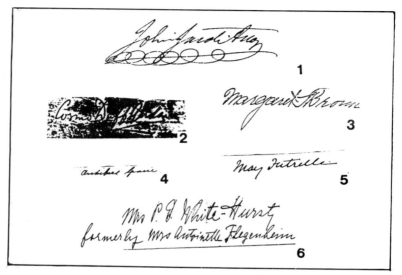

Figure 41

1. John Jacob Astor; multimillionaire, wealthiest passenger aboard.
2. Sir Cosmo Duff Gordon; the man accused of cowardice.
3. Margaret T. Brown, otherwise known as 'Unsinkable Molly'.
4. Colonel Archibald Gracie, author of best-selling book on the disaster, though he died before its publication.
5. Mrs. May Futrelle; widow of Jacques Futrelle, famous author of mystery stories.
6. Mrs. P.E. White-Hurst, formerly Mrs. Antoinette Flegenheim, who deposited almost 15,000 dollars worth of jewellery and cash in a Titanic safe, but never recovered the items!

No social discriminations have been made in those selected for analysis. The samples featured here and in the next few pages are simply the handwritings which happen to have come my way.

All of the passengers whose signatures are illustrated above were travelling first class. Second and third class passengers will be featured in the next chapter.

1. As already mentioned, Astor was returning from a long, luxurious honeymoon with his young wife, Madeleine. After their extensive travels, she was already in what one might describe as a 'delicate condition'. The Colonel had not lost much time. But then, he would hardly be likely to do so . . . not with those huge, swirling undertones.

Technically, of course, those repeated, obsessive swirls ('curlicues', as some might describe them) could also be said to relate to his financial interest. A multi-millionaire, who was primarily responsible for the building of the Waldorf Astoria Hotel in New York, he was a very money-minded man.

That extraordinary signature also shows him to be egotistical to the point of megalomania. Had he been an actor, he would undoubtedly have taken centre stage — and held it.

The width of the signature is worth noting too.

People whose writing is as broad as this like to spread themselves without restriction; needing plenty of room and space to work. This sort of style is precisely what I would expect from a man of Col. Astor's stature. It shows him to have thought big, spent big, wined, dined and indulged his every whim and fancy.

He was not a man to pare down his life to the essentials. When he liked something, he liked it to excess — money, motor cars, food, drink and all the rest of life's luxuries. He can also be seen to have been a man of multifarious talents: artistic, creative, inventive. Everything he did would have been on a vast scale; and everyone in his circle would have known about it.

This writing truly reflects the style of the man who penned it, it shows how much he enjoyed living on a grand scale: reflecting his confidence, broadmindedness and self-assertiveness.

Unfortunately, only his signature is available, so we cannot compare it to the text of any writing he might have produced, to determine if he was the same in private as in public: to establish whether he was frank and friendly, or tactless and indiscreet - a fascinating individual, or a king-sized bore. Whichever he was, he was undoubtedly an amazing man: a real individual.

2. As an avid reader of anything remotely related to the Titanic, I have long held certain views about people connected with her demise. My change of opinion about Captain Lord of the Californian has already been recorded.

But what of Sir Cosmo Duff Gordon, a man accused of cowardice, bribery and worse?

Sir Cosmo was one of the few English passengers and the only true aristocrat aboard. (The Countess of Rothes and indeed, Lady Lucy

Duff Gordon can be discounted; both having married into their titles).

The Duff Gordons, who enjoyed the grand social occasions no less than the Astors, were making the trip for business reasons . . . Lady Lucy's business. She was a highly successful fashion designer, feted on both sides of the Atlantic for her brilliant designs. Her tea gowns were in ever-increasing demand and she was returning to New York after setting up a branch of Maison Lucile in Paris.

The only available passage, at short notice, was on Titanic. Her Ladyship was none too happy about making the trip on a new ship, so she talked her husband into accompanying her: something he would not normally have done, because the couple tended to follow their separate interests. He was the country gentleman (a Hooray Henry who had lost an eye in a shooting accident, poor chap). She was the social butterfly.

But how enchanted she must have been on stepping aboard, to see many of the lady passengers robed in the newest Spring fashions; some from her very own couture collection. The trip might be worth making after all, she must have decided.

So what foul deed did Sir Cosmo do to be labelled a blackguard and a cad?

Put simply, he was in the wrong place at the wrong time.

Specifically, when the fate of that beautiful ship became apparent, he clambered with his lady and her maid, into a lifeboat. Number One lifeboat, as it happened.

Accompanied by two American businessmen, two seamen and five firemen, they sailed away into the sunrise . . . a total of twelve people, with room for at least thirty more to share their craft.

But the seats remained empty.

Small talk in the lifeboat got around to clothes (as it inevitably would, with Lady Lucy on board) and a member of crew happened to mention having lost all his kit on the sinking ship. Sir Cosmo, feeling sorry for the seamen (or so he claimed), offered to give him and his six friends new uniforms.

He kept his word. Cheques were duly made out to Symons, Henrickson, Taylor, Collins, Pusy, Sheath and Horswill. They were handed over shortly after His Lordship was hauled up, with his little contingent, onto the rescue ship, Carpathia.

His accusers put an entirely different interpretation on the action of the aristocrat. One of the seamen later stated that, when they attempted to turn back their half-empty lifeboat, with the express purpose of taking in more survivors from the water, Lady Lucy forbade them to do so, saying that they would be swamped.

The seamen claimed that Sir Cosmo upheld his wife's observation and that the £5 cheques were a bribe to encourage the crew to ignore the cries of the poor souls struggling in the water begging so pitifully for help. The Duff Gordons, it was alleged, urged the crew to row on, instead, to safety.

A most reprehensible act if it were true.

Was Sir Cosmo's generosity in making those payments deplorable, or naive in the extreme? What has his real motivation behind writing the cheques? We shall soon see.

Cast your eye back briefly to his signature.

The first impression is that it is a stylish hand, the hand of a man who was intelligent and cultured. But it does suggest that he had something to hide. Secrecy is manifest in the blackened loops and bizarre letter formations.

But what he was hiding was nothing more sinister than his own inadequacy. Sublimation figures strongly in this sample. The man was completely under the thumb of a more dominant force . . . presumably the lovely Lady Lucy.

Sexual frustration and repression manifest themselves in the formation of so many letters. Heavier vertical than horizontal strokes inevitably suggest a writer who longs, but fails, to be boss. The unfortunate man appears to have been unfulfilled and neglected.

Devotion to his wife was clearly Sir Cosmo's downfall. He was a weak and vulnerable character; foolish in the extreme. But he was not an evil man . . . one could say that his bark was worse than his bite. Sir Cosmo's main fault was to allow himself to be influenced and manipulated. A wretched soul; he could not possibly have foreseen the misery he would bring to himself as well as to others.

His general unpopularity appears to have been related to his offputting manner and attitudes. After all, his was not the only craft with empty seats. In the lifeboats which left Titanic on that dark night there were, apparently, 432 unfulfilled places.

Sir Cosmo Duff Gordon was, I submit, as much a victim of circumstances as — in their different ways — were Mr. Bruce Ismay and Captain Stanley Lord.

Having seen his writing, I can only conclude that his wife was the real miscreant. (Unfortunately, I have been unable to obtain samples of her writing to confirm the observation).

3. With her big, bold writing, Margaret T. Brown made sure people knew when she was around. What a lot can be detected from that signature. Rounded letter tops and slight rightward slant tell us that she was a very warm-hearted person, who had the effect of making people love, or loathe her.

The pressure of this writing is relatively light. Combined with its large size, it suggests that the lady could rant and rave like a thunderstorm, but when her tantrum had ended and the storm subsided, so too would the effects of them. This was not a person to sulk, or to bear grudges. There is no malice in her signature.

And yet, there was much more to Mrs. Brown that met the eye. The clue is in that downward-pointing 't' bar — suggesting that although she could breathe fire and brimstone when the fancy took her, mostly she kept her emotions under control. Likewise her basest desires.

She had a strong sense of right and wrong. The structure of the 'r's' suggests a curious nature. She may well have been called a busybody. But her nosiness was not intended for purposes of prying: more to determine the nature of people's troubles, in order to try and help them. Margaret T. Brown's nature might have been described as 'bumptious' and she may have been something of a Nosey Parker, but she meant well and there was no real harm in her. The old head was screwed on the right way.

A blunt sort of person, she would have been in the habit of speaking her thoughts. If people did not like her, she may well have told them to 'get to the back of the queue' or some such. This woman had a style all her own. I like her.

4.   The reduction in size of Colonel Gracie's signature has no real bearing on the outcome. For it is the RELATIVE rather than the ACTUAL size which is of interest to the graphologist; i.e., the size of the middle zone in relation to upper and lower. In this case, the middle zone is small. Whereas small may not always be beautiful, it is almost always good.

The Colonel's hand is fast, mature, intellectual, if somewhat emotionally repressed. The signature was penned shortly after the sinking. It shows the control of the military man; the courage and the inner strength which enabled him to survive the hazards of the Atlantic and enabled him to press on just long enough to produce his excellent account of the event.

5.   Poor Mrs. Futrelle. Hers is such a cultured and lovely hand, but so sad. Deprived of her beloved and enormously popular husband, she appears to be devastated, but trying to make the best of her now so empty life.

The 'M' starts off bravely . . . a large, dominant letter, it leads into an equally well outline 'a'; but once she reaches the 'y', the revealing downstroke shows all too clearly what are her feelings on the severance of intimate relations. But, one can almost hear her say to herself that 'life must go on'.

The lady's tenacity is seen in the prolonged 's' and matching 't'bar. Here we have a neat little hand from a neat little lady, who is doing her best to put on a brave face for the sake of those left behind.

6.   What a dreadful state the unfortunate Mrs. White-Hurst was in when she signed this note. How the effects of that abominable April night must have seared themselves into her mind.

The signature shows her to have been suffering from a severe form of clinical depression. If she sought happiness and a fresh start through a second marriage and failed in the attempt, it was hardly the fault of her new husband.

The lady's writing manifests the deep-rooted effect the events of April 1912 had on her, both physiologically and psychologically. She must have been approaching mental breakdown when this sample was written. The evidence: an over-abundance of ink spots and pen trails.

These occur in cases of sheer physical and mental exhaustion. To explain why, imagine for a moment that you are returning from a shopping expedition and are overburdened with bags and baggage. Half a mile walk separates the shops from your home and no transport is available. You have to walk. With every step, the purchases seem to grow heavier and heavier.

They must be regularly placed down to rest the arms. Eventually, with all your strength and energies dissipated you may be capable of nothing more than dragging the heavy shopping along behind you. So it is with the mind.

When it reaches that stage of exhaustion, the motor mechanisms and neural pathways connecting the brain with the hand and thus controlling the pen's movement, act in similar fashion. They have the effect of making the writer drop the pen onto the page (ink spots) and drag it along the paper (pen trails). All of this happens in just a fraction of a second; just long enough to produce those tell-tale signs.

The evidence, as I say, is there in the lady's signature for all to see. Even with the naked eye, we can detect a host of ink spots . . . at the top of the 'H' in Hurst, after the 'y' in formerly; several times around the 'F'. The ink trails are more apparent still — down the capital 'E'; down the left side of the 't' in White, along the 'e' also in White; at the end of the ''t' in Hurst.

I weep for this writer and only hope she received the professional help she so desperately needed; because beneath all that sorrow was a person of real refinement: of class and quality. If only she could have given vent to her emotions instead of bottling them up the sake of good breeding . . . .

Edith Russell (listed as Miss Rosenbaum on Titanic's passenger list) was one of the survivors. This specimen of her writing (figure 40), penned forty six years after the event, is a classical example of garland letter connections; characterised by m's and n's shaped like

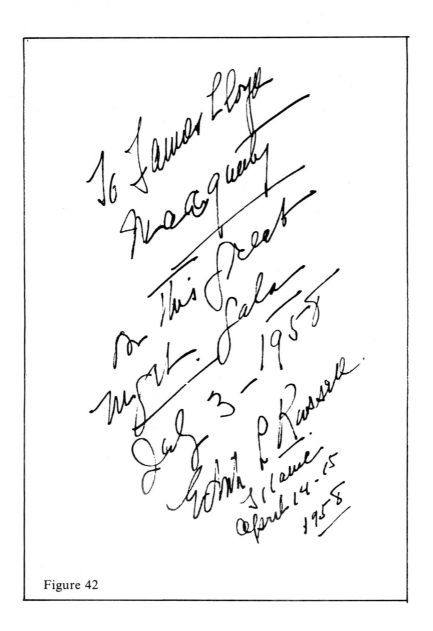

Figure 42

w's and u's. The whole tone of her script and its general layout show her to have been a woman of style and taste. The huge writing in this type of hand points to a longing for greatness (which, presumably, because of her experience she managed to achieve).

Miss Russell's writing is of a high form level, showing her to have been very positive, self-assertive and disciplined. The lady loved luxury and gracious living and was mighty imperious. Volatile too. Note all the 'temper ticks' and heavy strokes (at the beginning of the n in 'night', at the end of the t bars, and so on). She was not one to have her views challenged.

But she does manage to trip herself up: particularly in the execution of the word 'Titanic', which she writes rather differently from those surrounding it. For a start, that most significant work of all is the smallest on the page. It is also disjointed: and, if we take the line and full stop to follow her surname, rather than interpret them as a t bar and i dot, then that too is an important graphological sign. - The breaks in the word (which are not seen elsewhere) show an element of doubt in the memories surrounding Titanic. The fact that she has not paid attention to detail in writing the word suggests she may not have paid as much attention to the details surrounding the sinking as she later claimed to have done.

This grand old lady may have been respected for her charm and her elegance; with both of which she was undoubtedly well endowed. But her journey on and dramatic departure from the beleagured ship are a different matter; those memories seem to have been playing tricks with her. Yet few would challenge such an intimidating and imperious person. A purring tigress is best left that way.

Two other passengers must be included in our 'First Class' section . . . William Thomas Stead and a girl called Millie (no connection between them; as already explained, they were samples which happened to come into my possession.)

Stead's story is particularly sad: at least I think so. A man of vision, he refused to accept not only the prophetic utterances of others, but the evidence of his own 'inner eye'.

Stead had a lifelong interest in clairvoyance and psychic phenomena. The British journalist, editor, author, publisher and social reformer was renowned as a man with strong, precognitive powers. So strong were his psychic abilities that he had written descriptively about ships foundering in circumstances very similar to the Titanic . . . Not once had he done this, but twice; in each case many years before the disaster in which he was to lose his life.

Twenty six years previously . . . .

The Pall Mall Gazette published his fictitious story about a mail steamer sinking in mid-Atlantic with great loss of life, due to a shortage of lifeboats.

Twenty years previously . . . .

In the Review of Reviews, he wrote of a ship hitting an iceberg, also in mid-Atlantic.

Twenty four HOURS previously . . . .

No, that little tale can hold for a page or two.

William Thomas Stead was given many signs of impending catastrophe as time wore on. A variety of mystics and mediums, seers and visionaries warned him to keep away from water. Uncharacteristically, he ignored them all. But then, he had important work to do.

The President of America had issued a personal invitation to him to address an international Peace Conference. It was to be held at Carnegie Hall, on April 21; just three days after Titanic's estimated date of arrival in New York.

It would take more than the odd premonition or gypsy's warning to prevent him from fulfilling that sort of engagement. Stead settled down happily to enjoy his trip: which he did, for the first few days. Then, on the Saturday night, something happened which disturbed him greatly. His own precognitive powers surfaced from the depths of his unconscious to give him a short, sharp shock.

William Stead had a dream: an uncanny dream with a timeless quality, featuring hundreds of cats. They were being thrown from a high window to uncertain territory below. The dream haunted him throughout the next day, making him wonder if reality and illusion were merging together; if the present and the future were being rolled into one. It was most disconcerting.

With the memory of his dream still fresh in his mind, Stead related its details to his companions over dinner on Sunday. The oysters, smoked salmond and pate de fois gras must have stuck a little in the throats of those who listened. The story was not something to be taken with a pinch of salt. Old Stead was quite a raconteur and could put the fear of God into his audience if he wanted to. This time though, it was immediately apparent to his fellow diners that he was not having them on. The white bearded Spiritualist was frightened and he was not ashamed to admit it.

Nor could he shake off his feelings of foreboding.

Whether he interpreted the symbolism of cats being thrown from a high window to represent humans leaping from high decks and portholes, history does not record. But his instincts must have told him that, soon now, his fate and that of many of his fellow passengers would be sealed.

The first letter, written just three days before he was due to set off, has a dismissive tone. Like many journalists, Stead must have

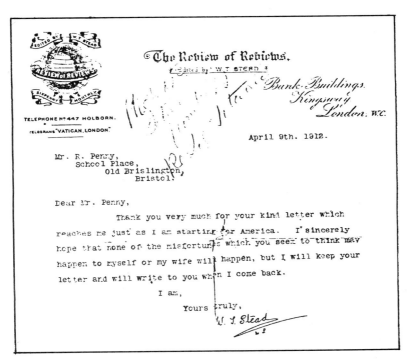

The Review of Reviews.
Edited by W.T STEAD

Bank Buildings.
Kingsway
London. W.C.

TELEPHONE Nº 447 HOLBORN.
TELEGRAMS "VATICAN, LONDON."

April 9th. 1912.

Mr. R. Penny,
School Place,
Old Brislington,
Bristol.

Dear Mr. Penny,

Thank you very much for your kind letter which reaches me just as I am starting for America. I sincerely hope that none of the misfortunes which you seem to think may happen to myself or my wife will happen, but I will keep your letter and will write to you when I come back.

I am,

Yours truly,
W. J. Stead

Figure 43

received his share of letters from what we scribes are almost too eager to dismiss as 'cranks'. His reply is polite, but curt. He has not even signed the letter, but has asked someone else (a secretary?) to do so on his behalf.

Before catching sight of the genuine Stead autograph, I had dismissed this one as being far too mousy to have belonged to a man of such charisma.

The second letter, (though chronologically, with its 1880 dateline it is the earlier of the two) is much more in keeping with William Stead's personality. It has a lovely, natural flow, is well spaced, balanced and rhythmical. The middle zone is small in relation to the upper and lower; confirming his interest in matters intellectual and spiritual — with above average attention being paid to 'leg activities'. Despite his advancing years, he was quite a boy, old William.

That loop to the left of the capital L points to an element of personal vanity. Delta d's epsilon e's confirm his literary talents. The way other letters diminish at the end hints at discretion and diplomacy.

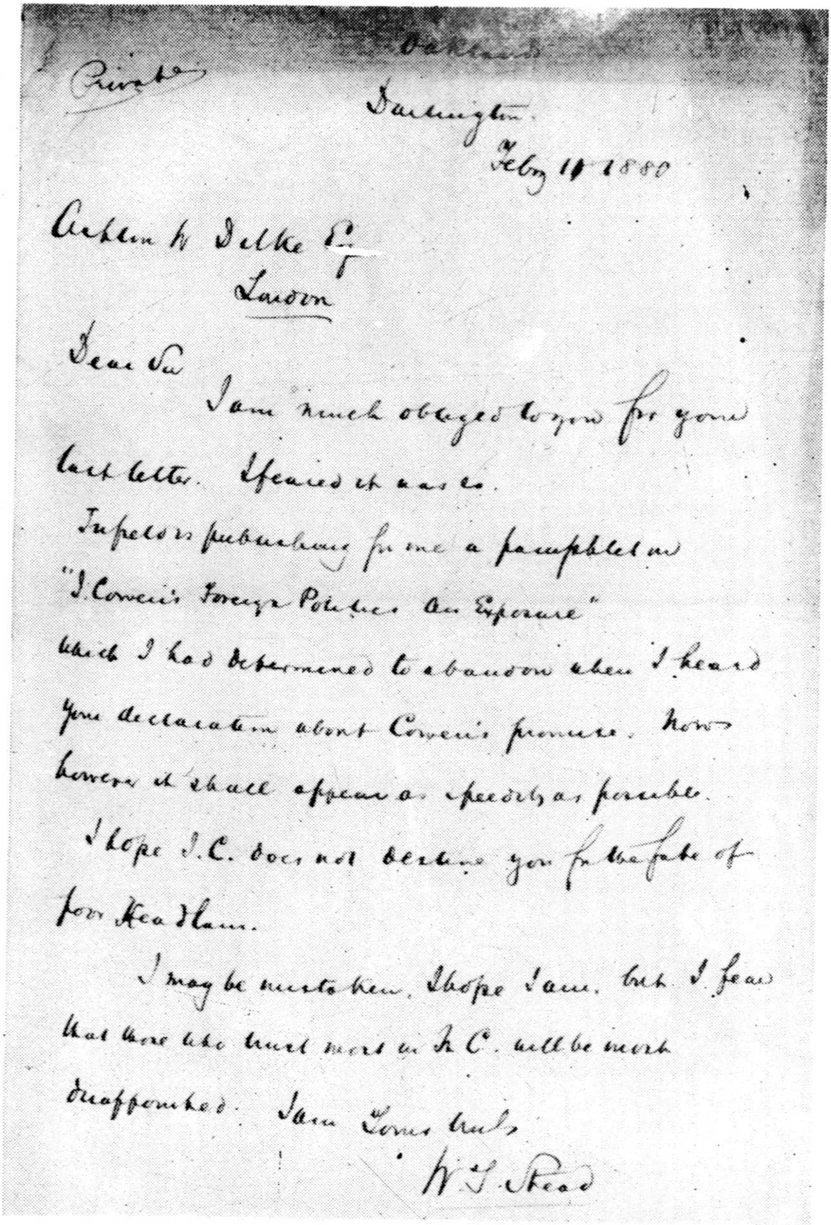

Oakland

Darlington.

Feby 14 1880

Arthur W Dilke Esq
London

Dear Sir

I am much obliged to you for your
last letter. I feared it was so.

I appear to be publishing for me a pamphlet on
"I. Cowen's Foreign Policies an Exposure"
which I had determined to abandon when I heard
your declaration about Cowen's promise. Now
however it shall appear as speedily as possible.

I hope I.C. does not deceive you for the fate of
poor Headlam.

I may be mistaken, I hope I am, but I fear
that those who trust most in I.C. will be most
disappointed. I am Yours truly,

W T Stead

Figure 44

Figure 45

I have slept on the dining room floor both nights, and we had a most awful thunder storm last night and today its that foggy. I shall be glad to be on Terra firma again.

We had a bad start, the New York broke adrift and ran into us at Southampton, well I wont write any more now, will you let Aunt Em and Nell, or anyone you think read this as I dont feel like going all over it again, and dont worry about me as I shall be well looked after and Ive made several well to do friends on board

lots of love to all
from your loving daughter
Millie.

First letter home   Ap 29th

The baseline is level until he signs off when it drops considerably. This, I would attribute to tiredness and overwork: a common failing among writers. Poor William Stead.

Why did he have to go on that trip, even if his friend the President was — as we must assume — paying the fare? It must go down in history as the 'freebie' to end all 'freebies' . . . .

Millie was the maid of Mr. and Mrs. Hudson J. Allison of Montreal. Her duties were to care for their two small children, Lorraine was three years old and Trevor, the baby. When the danger was at its height and women and children were being ordered into the lifeboats, Mrs. Allison handed her infant son over to the maid. Like Mrs. Straus, this devoted wife was also determined to stay with her husband. Her small daughter was equally determined to stay with her mother. Lorraine clung desperately to the flowing skirts and nothing would induce her to let go.

So Millie took baby Trevor as instructed, while the rest of the family perished.

In her 'first letter home', the maid witholds certain information from her parents . . . presumably to spare their feelings. The blacking in of several letters (notably the smal! 'e's'), show how she is unconsciously blocking out certain memories, even from herself: which is perfectly understandable in the circumstances.

Note too, how clearly she writes those very significant words: 'I don't feel like going all over it again'.

This is a more articulate and educated hand than one would expect from the average servant girl of the period.

Mr. and Mrs. Allison had trained her well.

After all . . . how many girls in service would use the Latin words 'terra firma'?

There is considerably more to Millie than meets the eye.

HANDS OFF THE TITANIC

CHAPTER TEN:
Second and third class

Chapter Ten: Second and Third Class

Baron Alfred Drachstedt boarded Titanic with a second class ticket; but no sooner had he set foot on the magnificent floating palace that he decided second class was not for him. So he took himself to the purser's office, paid the difference and switched to first class accommodation . . . which, one must admit, was more in keeping with a titled gentleman.

However, the 'Baron' was not what he appeared to be. He was actually a commoner; albeit one with Teutonic bearing. But a commoner, just the same. His real name was plain old Alfred Nourney. Why he should want to adopt a name so similar to that of Count Dracula is anyone's guess. Was it a deliberate attempt to 'take the mickey'? We shall soon see.

Another second class passenger whose writing is about to be examined is Lawrence Beesley, science master at Dulwich College, London, who — like Col. Gracie — survived to write a book about the event but who — unlike the Colonel — did see his work published, re-published and lived on to enjoy fame and much literary success.

We shall also meet Pastor Harper (lost), Mrs. F. Angle (saved), Mr. H. Denbury (lost), Mr. R. Phillips (lost). From the third class section come Eugene Daly (saved), Ed Ryan (saved) and a child called Mabel (lost?). Mystery surrounds little Mabel, as we shall see. But first, let us look at what 'the Baron' has to say; or, more to the point, how he goes about saying it. Here we have not just one signature; but both of them.

What an odd sort of fellow the 'Baron' appears to have been. With all those blacked out letters, changes of emphasis and other 'banana slips' in the mind, he strikes me as being the sort of scoundrel with whom no self-respecting father would trust his daughter. His writing is totally lacking in warmth. But he is keen and has excellent powers of comprehension. His heavy strokes reveal his strong sense of colour and style. A very individualistic sort of person: the type who, with his persuasive line of patter and beautiful manners, could charm the snakes out of the grass. Personally, I find him enchanting . . . his writing suggests he was a real, loveable rogue.

He also appears to have been a first rate comic and impersonator. A real ladies' man: the life and soul of the party, even if it WAS a big act.

His writing is that of a man who enjoyed moving in exalted circles. He would have been excellent company, but those repressed and inhibited upper loops tell us that if anyone was foolish enough to try and get close to him, up would go the mental barriers; 'Drachstedt'

110

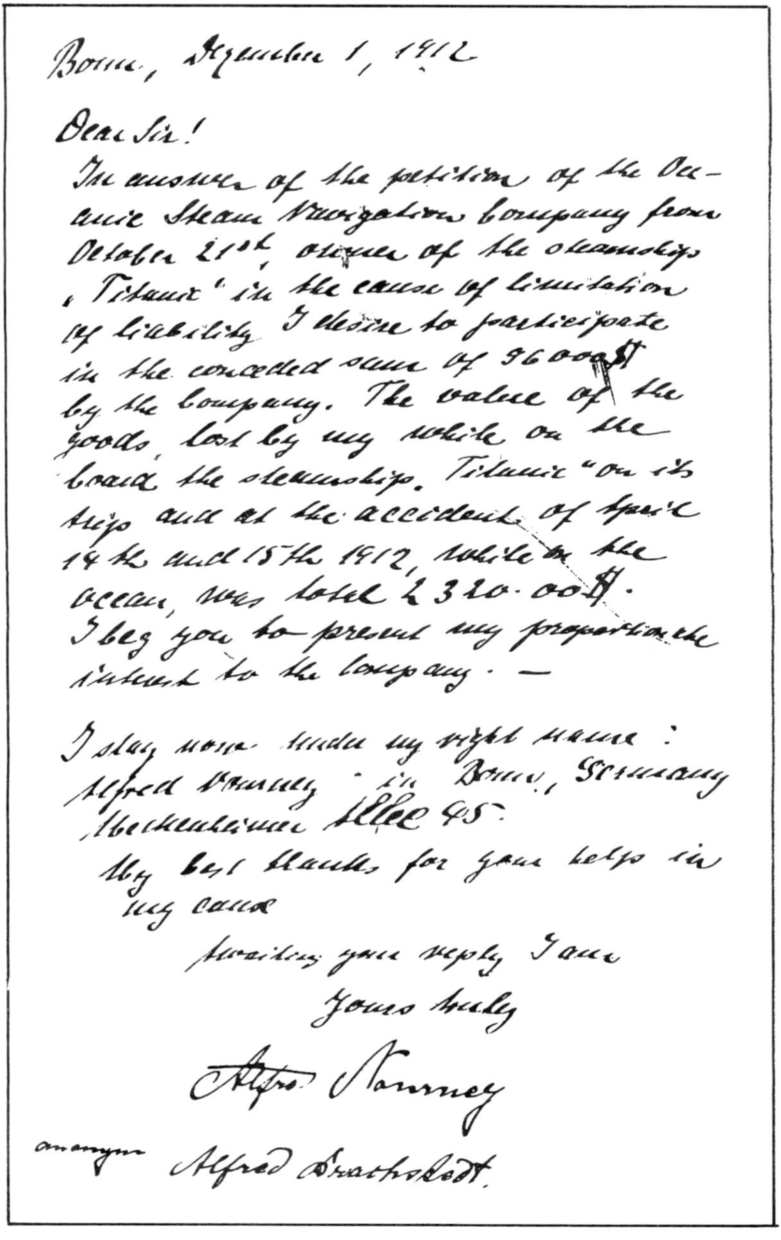

Bonn, December 1, 1912

Dear Sir!

In answer of the petition of the Oceanic Steam Navigation Company from October 21st, owner of the steamship "Titanic" in the cause of limitation of liability, I desire to participate in the conceded sum of 96000$ by the company. The value of the goods, lost by me while on the board the steamship "Titanic" on its trip and at the accident of April 14th and 15th 1912, while in the ocean, was total £320.00$.

I beg you to present my proportionate interest to the company. —

I stay more under my right name: Alfred Drancey in Bonn, Germany, Herwarthstrasse Allee 45.

My best thanks for your helps in my cause

awaiting your reply I am

Yours truly

Alfd. Drancey

anonym Alfred Drathsledt.

Figure 47

111

would retreat into his shell, possibly taking refuge in heavy sarcasm on the way.

He loved luxury and his writing suggests he would have been a most flamboyant and snazzy dresser. A self satisfied, smug and conceited man, he was not the sort to confide in others. Why?

Because of a very basic inadequacy within him . . . an inadequacy of which only he knew — and now I know. So you would all like to know too. Well, I'm sorry, but I don't think it would be fair to expose the Baron's best kept secret.

Not when he went to such pains to conceal it. Far be it for me to pass on juicy bits of gossip. Graphologists have their code of ethics too, you know.*

All I can say is that poor dear Freddie had certain problems in relation to . . . well, er . . . relationships. And, in common with most people who suffer from such inadequacies, he felt the urge to behave like the true exhibitionist he was.

A complete sham?

Of course he was. But he meant no harm. His mischievous sense of fun was what motivated him. Think of the entertainment he must have provided on board. There would never have been a dull moment with this character around. And, when the crunch came, he would have risen splendidly to the occasion. I have no doubt that he would have done all in his power to brighten those darkest hours before the dawn . . . .

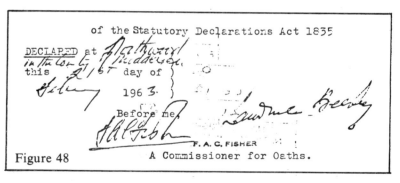

Figure 48

For Lawrence Beesley, 25 year old science master at Dulwich College, the journey was being made in his Easter holiday from school. He was travelling second class in cabin: D.56, near the dining saloon.

Beesley escaped in a lifeboat (number 13) and subsequently wrote a book which provided a graphic account of his experiences.*[10] The first edition, published in 1912, was so successful that the second edition appeared just three months later.

The signature reproduced here is taken from a statutory declaration for use in the campaign to clear the name of Captain Lord. It comes to me courtesy of Leslie Harrison and Beesley was eighty seven years old at the time this document was signed, sealed and delivered.

Though still alert, it would appear from certain letter formations (notably the pointed top of the lower case 'l'), that he had experienced much emotional stress and physical pain. It was as if the events of that April night so many decades earlier were still fresh in his mind.

Even in his advancing years, Beesley was still the sort of man who liked to behave in an organised and disciplined way. The small middle zone and sharp outlines harp back to the scientific leanings of his youth. The events of that night were anything but neat and tidy.

Despite all that, Beesley got by. He was in his ninetieth year when he died in 1967. . .

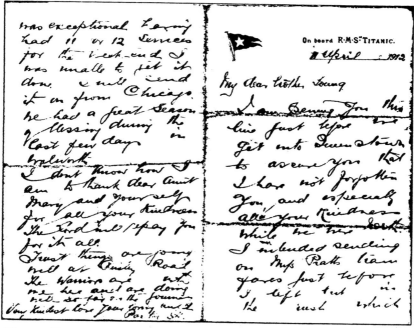

Figure 49

Now for an autographed letter on official Titanic writing paper, from Pastor Harper. The man comes through as being a quick thinker, alert, perceptive. Fast flowing thoughts are seen in the way all the letters are joined together. The backward pull shows the importance he attached to tradition (leftward swing on the y tail, capital T and capital I . . . which latter sign suggests that the dominant influence in his youth was that of his father).

This is the strong, positive hand of a man who was genuinely good, kind, altruistic.

Sadly, Pastor Harper was lost, but not before seeing to it that his daughter Nina and niece Jessie who were travelling with him were both saved . . .

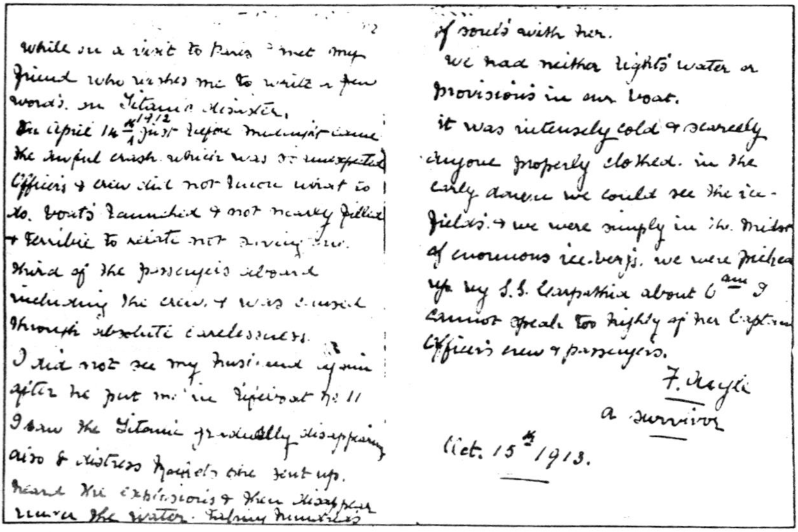

Figure 50

Eighteen months after the sinking, Mrs. Angle, who lost her husband on that awful April night, wrote this letter.

Clearly, the unfortunate woman was deeply affected by the tragedy. The writing is fractured and falling apart. Symbolically, it is as if her very life were doing the same . . .

The following is another letter written aboard; this one in sight of the Irish coast, by Mr. Herbert Denbury.

I am not too happy about Mr. Denbury. His writing is full of mental 'banana slips' . . . there is a liberal sprinkling of extra letters, covering strokes and oddly-shaped words.

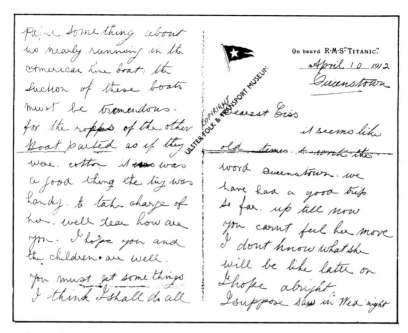

Figure 51

The extra letters, which can be seen by the naked eye, appear on page one — line 7, 'can't'; page two, line 5 'tremendous'; line 6 'ropes'; line 7, 'was'; line 8 'thing'; last line 'think'. These all give the impression of some sort of cover up . . . as if he was not completely straight with his darling Cissie.

Word spacing is irregular and there is a very stubborn streak to be seen in those final strokes of the end letters; as if, symbolically, he were digging his heels in.

An argumentative and unpleasant type, Mr. Denbury. His writing contains many signs of irritation and confusion.

Sorry, but this one is far too negative for my taste . . .

Robert Phillips, like Pastor Harper, saved his daughter, but not himself. Mr. Phillips wrote the postcard illustrated overleaf.

Ignore the ink blot. That would be due to vibration on the ship . . . or to someone having accidentally bumped into him. The writing itself is of a high form level; its heavy pastiness showing Mr. Phillips to have been very emotional.

Figure 52

He loved his daughter very much: note how large the initial letter of her name. Clearly, he thought the world of Alice.

Disjointed words suggest good intuitive powers. Although it is not possible to judge age from one's writing, this man does seem to be past the first flower of youth — and it might be interesting to know that the Ulster Folk and Transport Museum paid £2,000 for the original version of this postcard.

Michael McCaughan, the museum's maritime historian and author told me:

"We originally thought we held the world record for the dearest postcard sold at the Titanic auction of memorabilia, but later discovered another card had cost twice as much."

The auction was held at the Park Lane Hotel in London, on April 15 1987; the 75th Anniversary of the ship's sinking. . .

Figure 53 *Eugene Daly*

Eugene Daly is something of an enigma. His is a cultured and aesthetic hand: that of a man who was well-educated, albeit without funds (otherwise, would he have been travelling steerage?).

The flamboyant 'E', with which he starts his signature and the unusual 'y' with which he ends it, suggest he was a great one for 'making an entrance . . . and an exit'.

If he hadn't been playing his pipes, he would surely have been putting on some other act: singing, dancing or showing off to the multitudes. The 'entrance' he certainly did make, by striking up a mournful ditty on his bagpipes to an audience of passengers he probably did not even trouble to consult first.

The sound of the instrument would have drowned out their objections, anyway. He was fortunate not to have made his 'exit' on the trip; though he and his pipes were parted at some stage.

(Did they fall, or were they pushed overboard?). Whichever, he subsequently claimed fifty dollars from the shipping company to cover the loss.

A bit of a dark horse, this Irishman. No pun is intended, if I say his writing shows him to have been a still water that ran very deep.

He was quite a religious type too. This 'd' is often seen in the hands of 'cradle Catholics', which Eugene would almost certainly have been. Indeed, if he and his beastly bagpipes had not separated, he strikes me as being the sort of chap who would have been insensitive enough to have played the hymn which so many people argue about . . . given half a chance, this morose little man would have followed Erin's Lament with Nearer My God to Thee.

His writing reminds me very much of that of a neurotic priest who was once a fellow passenger with me on a flight to Rome.

As we were about to take off, he crossed himself and called out to those in the surrounding seats:

'And now, let us pray for a safe take-off . . . and a happy death . . .'

Did the well-meaning, but misguided Eugene Daly have the same effect on his fellow passengers? I wonder . . .

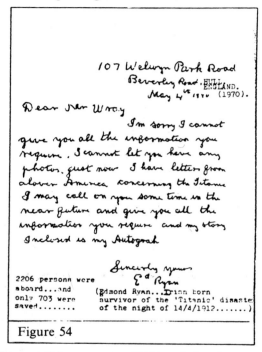

107 Welwyn Park Road
Beverley Road, HULL,
ENGLAND.
May 4th 1970 (1970).

Dear Mr Wrdy

I'm sorry I cannot give you all the information you require. I cannot let you have any photos just now. I have letters from a lover America concerning the Titanic I may call on you some time in the near future and give you all the information you require and my story Inclosed is my Autograph

Sincerely yours
E d Ryan

2206 persons were aboard...and only 703 were saved........

(Edmond Ryan...Irish born survivor of the 'Titanic' disaste of the night of 14/4/1912.......)

Figure 54

Patrick Ryan and his young son Ed boarded at Queenstown. As in the previous two cases cited, the father was lost, the child saved.

Ed Ryan was fortunate. Fewer than a third of the children travelling steerage were given places in the lifeboats.

The letter reproduced here was written many years later, when Ed Ryan was quite elderly.

It is a very taut and restricted hand; but honest and totally lacking in pretentiousness. The most interesting point about this letter is the manner in which the word 'America' drops below those surrounding it, as if, even fifty eight years after the event, memories of going there are still tinged with sorrow . . . .

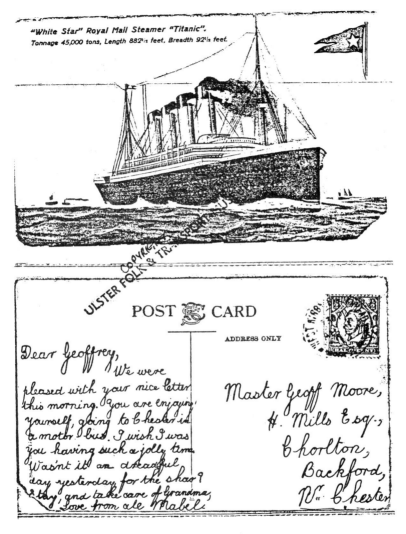

"White Star" Royal Mail Steamer "Titanic".
Tonnage 45,000 tons, Length 882½ feet, Breadth 92½ feet.

POST CARD

ADDRESS ONLY

Dear Geoffrey,
We were pleased with your nice letter this morning. You are enjoying yourself, going to Chester in a motor bus. I wish I was you having such a jolly time. Wasn't it an dreadful day yesterday for the shar? Stay, and take care of Grandma. Love from ole Mabel

Master Geoff Moore,
H. Mills Esq.,
Chorlton,
Backford,
N' Chester

Figure 55

Who is Mabel? This charmingly immature hand sent me searching through the records to find any young person of that name and there, in the list provided at the back of Walter Lord's book*[11] I found among the third class passengers who perished, one 'Mabel Skoog, child': so I could only assume this was she.

What a delightful poppet she must have been. Beautifully neat and tidy. It is never easy to analyse children's hands because they have not yet broken away from the copybook style taught at school; at least, not usually enough to strike their note of individuality. This writer had not matured sufficiently for an in-depth analysis to be conducted. She was still doing precisely what she was told; minding her manners and behaving impeccably. It seemed that the poor little mite's only fault was that she was travelling steerage and was therefore lost.

Had she been a first or second class passenger, she would surely have been saved. Records show that only one first class child died that night. Lorraine, the three year old daughter of Mr. and Mrs. Hudson J. Allison, clung to the skirts of her mother who chose, like Mrs. Straus (see page 120) to stay on the Titanic with her husband. Steerage children totalled seventy six — of whom, fifty three died.

So who was this mysterious Mabel?

John P. Eaton, one of the founder members of the Titanic Historical Society, who has served as its historian since its inception tells me:-

"Mabel Skoog, aged nine, embarked with her family at Southampton. She was Swedish and travelling to meet her uncle, Olaus Ras, of Iron Mountain, Michigan, USA. Her name is not on the list of those saved."

Eaton could offer no explanation as to why a little Swedish girl, on such a trip, should take it upon herself to write to anyone in the heart of Cheshire — and neither could I.

Mystery surrounded little Mabel. A graphologist need not do much 'detective' work to conclude that this handwriting is not that of someone brought up in Sweden: or, if it is, then it is heavily influenced by a British tutor. And that is, as the Americans might say 'a whole new ball game'.

Why should a Scandinavian child, tutored by an English person, be so impoverished as to have to travel steerage? Who was she travelling with? Did she ask another child to write this postcard on her behalf?

Then it occured to me that perhaps this Mabel was not Mabel Skoog at all, but another child of the same name? But if that were so, where on the records was there another Mabel listed? Again, John P.

Eaton, normally such a mine of information, could come up with nothing tangible.

'Take care of grandma' implores the writer of this postcard. Was there no-one to take care of Mabel, I found myself wondering.

And there this sorry little tale might have ended were it not for the concluding comment of Michael McCaughan, purchaser of the postcard, who had no idea I had been off on a wild goose chase.

"This particular Mabel had nothing to do with Titanic, I'm afraid. The card was postmarked 1st August, 1912."

In the aftermath of the tragedy, thousands of Titanic postcards were printed and correspondents regularly sent them to each other: for their curiosity value, presumably.

The moral of this tale?

Graphologists should beware of jumping to conclusions. It is all too easy to end up with egg (or, in this case, ice) on the face.

*[10]   The Loss of the SS Titanic by Lawrence Beesley, originally published by Houghton Miffin Co. (1912)
*[11]   A Night to Remember, by Walter Lord, Longman Green & Co. (1956); Penguin (1987)

Footnote:

Claes-Göran Wetterholm took issue with me on the subject of 'the Baron'. "It is unfair to torment people like this. Reading about him made me curious. Other readers might also want to know what was the matter with 'the Baron'. Please explain."

So, for the benefit of Claes-Göran and others who would like to know, I can reveal that the unfortunate chap's problems were of a very personal nature. Showman though he was, the evidence suggests that he was impotent.

HANDS OFF THE TITANIC

CHAPTER ELEVEN:

Rescuers . . . and others

Chapter Eleven: Rescuers . . . and Others

Figure 56

Captain Arthur Rostron of the RMS Carpathia was the man who rushed to the scene of the disaster; picked up Titanic survivors and was proclaimed an international hero for ever more.

Certainly, his writing shows him to be alert and quick thinking. The analysis is based not only on the signature reproduced above, but also on a confidential letter to his employers, which I am not at liberty to reproduce. There is much grace and elegance in this hand. Wide, inter-word spacing indicates independence and other signs suggest that he was a first rate organiser; which indeed proved to be the case when it came to accommodating all those unexpected extra passengers aboard his vessel. His writing shows initiative and hints at a responsive, emotional nature. The underscore in a positive hand like this shows self-reliance (in a negative hand it has a rather different interpretation, as we shall see).

But he was also an eccentric man (notice the odd 'e' in the word 'master') and stubborn with it. Certain signs in this signature suggest he could be curt; rude even. There are indications that he was in the habit of ending friendships as abruptly as he formed them. . .

Figure 57

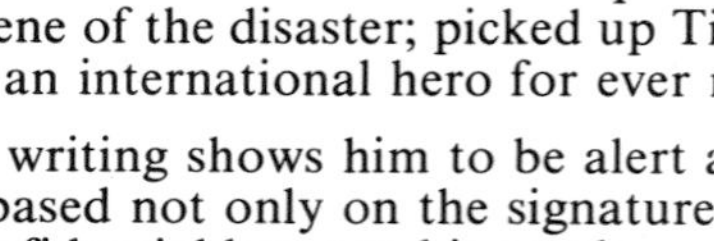

George E. Stewart was the Californian's chief officer: Captain Lord's second in command: a mature, confident type, according to his signature. Again, those disjointed letters hint at strong intuitive powers and suggest he was one for playing hunches. His writing shows him to have been strongly ambitious, bright and helpful. The long 't' bars denote enthusiasm and optimism, their upward movement showing above-average determination to advance in his professional career. This is a self-possessed hand; good, positive.

In slant and letter structure, this could be said to bear certain similarities to the signature of Captain Smith; though Smith's is considerably more flamboyant.

In later life, perhaps the flamboyance would become more evident in the hand of George E. Stewart. I do not know, because I have no further samples of his writing.

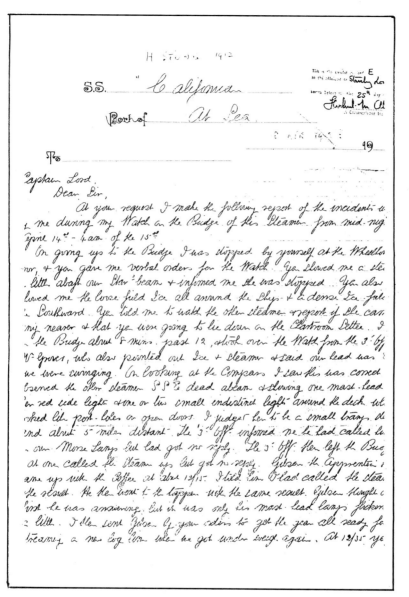

H. STONE 1912

S.S. "California"

Port of At Sea

19

To

Captain Lord,

Dear Sir,

At your request I make the following report of the incidents to + me during my Watch on the Bridge of this Steamer from mid-night April 14th – 4 am of the 15th.

On going up to the Bridge I was stopped by yourself at the Wheelhouse nr, + you gave me verbal orders for the Watch. You showed me a steamer little abaft our Star-beam + informed me she was stopped. You also showed me the loose field Ice all around the Ship + a dense Ice field to Southward. You told me to watch the other steamer + report if she came any nearer + that you were going to lie down on the Chartroom Settee. I — the Bridge about 8 mins. past 12, took over the Watch from the 3rd off W. Groves, who also pointed out Ice + steamer + said our head was + we were swinging. On looking at the Compass I saw this was correct observed the other steamer S.S.E. dead abeam + showing one mast-head + red side light + one or two small indistinct lights around the deck which looked like port-holes or open doors. I judged her to be a small tramp steamer + about 5 miles distant. The 3rd off informed me he had called her on our Morse Lamp but had got no reply. The 3rd off then left the Bridge at one called the steamer up but got no reply. Gibson the apprentice came up with the Coffee at about 12/15. I told him I had called the steamer + he started. He then went to the toppen with the same result. Gibson thought he saw he was answering but it was only his mast head lamp flicker a little. I then sent Gibson by your orders to get the gear all ready for stearing a new log line when he got under weigh again. At 12/35 you

So what became of him? Sadly, he was a casualty of the Second World War.

In March, 1940, a newspaper reported the death of a sixty two year old retired shipmaster who had, in the words of Leslie Harrison 'temporarily returned to sea as a third officer to oblige a friend, captain of the s.s. Barnhill.

'Off the Isle of Wight, German aircraft had bombed and sunk the ship. Lost was her third officer. His name — G.F. Stewart.'

'The address of the officer was given as Sale, in Cheshire. The age and the place were right. On reading the obituary notice, Captain Lord felt sure that this must have been the former chief officer of the Californian . . . as indeed he was.' . . .

Herbert Stone had a first mate's certificate and, although technically serving as second officer, became nominal first officer of the Californian. He was in charge of the watch on the night in question, while Captain Lord snatched a few hours rest.

Sure enough, Stone saw signals; but decided they were not the distress variety and that the ship he had seen was steaming away (which Titanic most certainly was not). After that, his story becomes confused and so does his writing.

At first glance, it seems consistent enough but there is a certain vulgarity about it. There is too much ornamentation, (note the unnecessary scrolls on most of the capitals — C, S, T, etc.); there are too many curlicues. And yet, despite the flashy signs, the underlying tone suggest a real lack of imagination. This writing is slow, ungainly, cramped. It is also boring: the product of a man old beyond his years . . . a dullard. However, one wonders, did he manage to pass the necessary examinations for his first mate's certificate? Herbert Stone was a tedious man, with little in the way of personality.

Yet he subsequently achieved much notoriety for himself by telling the most outrageous lies about his Captain. Why? Resentment perhaps. There is some evidence of it in his writing. Jealousy figures too. But I would not interpret that as his main problem. Drink is the more likely cause of the shaky writing portrayed here. Trembling downstrokes inevitably suggest a drink problem; particularly when combined with arcade connections.

This would account for his confused state of mind.

Under the influence of alcohol, some people can be very convincing story tellers!

Figure 59

126

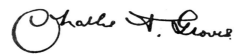

Figure 60

Charles V. Groves was Californian's Third Officer. As explained in chapter two, writing is divided into three zones: upper, middle and lower. An enlargement of any one of the three shows undue emphasis being placed in that particular direction. Groves' 1912 signature shows him to have been endowed with an overactive imagination. That odd 'c' hints at an element of jealousy; as if he resented the more important positions held by other officers. (What a delightful lot Californian's officers were!).

His 1959 signature suggests that the publicity to which he had been subjected over the years, had gone to his head . . . or perhaps it was simply that a man of his growing importance reflected this aspect of his personality in his writing. Whatever the reason, note the flamboyant C, unusual A; underscoring not just with a line or even two lines, but enhanced with curves and flourishes.

Groves was a show-off to the Nth degree . . . even as a septuagenarian, loving every minute of his centre stage position. What became of him after 1912?

Over to Leslie Harrison (and I quote from his book, A Titanic Myth, already referred to):

'Groves had a distinguished career in the Merchant Navy. After service in the Royal Naval Reserve in the First World War, he went into W.A. Souter's, shipowners based in Newcastle, where he attained command. After eleven years as a shipmaster, he was appointed marine superintendent, also serving on the marine superintendents' committee of the Chamber of Shipping.

'He was elected a Younger Brother of Trinity House and, by an interesting turn of fortune, in 1931 was appointed as a nautical assessor to serve on marine inquiries. In that capacity he had a reputation for being always a considerate and humane man. In the 1939—1945 war, he returned to service in the Royal Navy Reserve.'

Groves died in September 1961, just two years after penning the second signature featured above. He was aged seventy one at the time of writing it . . . .

On the fate of Stone, I cannot comment. I assume that, as he would now be getting on towards the age of one hundred and twenty, he is no longer living! but have no details of his date or place of death . . .

127

JAMES GIBSON 1912 ... F referred to ... Stanley Lord.

sworn before me this 25th day of June 1954

_____ Allen.

A Commissioner for Oaths.

April 18th 1912.

Captain Lord
    Dear Sir.

        In compliance with your wishes, I hereby make the following statement as to what I saw on the morning of April 15th 1911:-

        It being my watch on deck from 12 o'clock until 4 o'clock, I went on the bridge at about 15 minutes after twelve and saw that the ship was stopped and that she was surrounded with light field-ice & thick field-ice to the Southward. While the 2nd officer & I were having coffee, a few minutes later, I asked him if there were any more ships around us. He said that there was one on the Starboard beam, & looking over the weather-cloth, I saw a white light flickering which I took to be a morse light calling us up. I then went over to the key-board & gave one long flash in answer, & still seeing this light flickering, I gave her the calling up sign. The light on the other ship, however, was still the same, so I looked at her through the binoculars & found that it was her masthead light flickering, I also observed her port sidelight & a faint glare of lights on her afterdeck. I then went over to the 2nd officer & remarked that she looked like a tramp steamer. He said that most probably she was, & was burning oil lights. This ship was then right abeam. At about 25 minutes after twelve I went down off the bridge to get a new log out & not being able to find it, I went on the bridge again to see if the 2nd officer knew anything about it. I then noticed that this other ship was about one point & a half before the beam. I then went down again & was down until about 5 minutes to one. Arriving on the bridge again at that time, the 2nd officer told me that the other ship

Figure 61

128

On the night of the Titanic disaster, apprentice, James Gibson, was on deck. He was on watch duty from midnight until four a.m. He claimed that at 12.15 a.m., he saw a ship stopped to the south of the Californian and that she was surrounded by ice. He alleged that he saw flickering lights through his binoculars, but believed at the time, that the vessel he sighted was a tramp steamer rather than a passenger liner.

Later, he stated that it could have been a passenger line. Why he changed his story is anyone's guess. Confusion reigned in the mind of this apprentice, as is obvious from his writing.

His hand (like that of Stone) shows many inconsistencies. Both write with arcade letter connections, showing them to be men whose emotions rule their heads.

In the case of Gibson, although inter-word and inter-line spacings are regular enough, there is occasional intermingling of loops; confirming the observation about mental confusion (again, like Stone).

It is a secretive, pretentious and thoroughly awkward hand. Those elaborate capitals show a desire to impress. The cumbersome strokes and dominance of underlengths combine to reveal the writer's very materialistic nature. The lower loops are out of proportion to the left of the capitals (notably the S and I and L) point to personal vanity. His unnecessarily ornate capitals hint at vulgarity. The many concealing strokes and blacked out letters suggest that he had something to hide. He clearly did not have a high opinion of either his captain or his second officer. What ultimately became of him, I do not know, other than that his death occured in February, 1963, a year after that of his former captain.

Compare the size of the S in Sir with the D in Dear. Note too how tiny the symbol 2nd has become. He does not even accord this officer the courtesy of a capital O. Alright, so it is quite conventional for the words 'second officer' to be in lower case, I still think a little respect is called for. Allowing for the fact that this is an uneducated and therefore not very literate writer, the script contains more negative than positive signs.

Many people may have taken this foolish man seriously, but personally, I would question his integrity. . .

Benjamin Kirk's name has already arisen. His was the discharge book from which a page was reproduced in chapter one. Kirk was on lookout from 10.00 p.m. until midnight. He was on watch again at 4.00 a.m. At 6.00 a.m., on the morning after the sinking, he had the dubious honour of being hoisted up in a coal basket shackled to the mainmast stay with instructions to look for the Titanic.

He too used binoculars, but as we all now know, by then there was

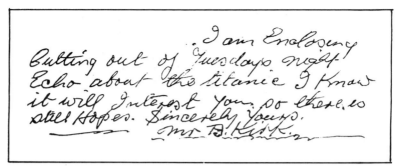

Figure 62

nothing to be seen (Titanic had disappeared from sight some three hours and forty minutes earlier).

Kirk was a good and trustworthy seaman, who spent many of his thirty five years at sea, serving with Captain Lord, whom he found considerate and understanding at all times.

Reproduced here is the closing paragraph of a letter Kirk wrote to Leslie Harrison in 1970. Kirk was then eighty years old and living at a residential home for elderly, retired seafarers in Wallasey; the town where Captain Lord had made his home.

It is an honest and straightforward hand; its somewhat shaky style I would attribute to age and deteriorating health. Nevertheless, it still reflects the writer's qualities, showing him to be regular, reliable and a man who was not likely to have his opinion swayed in any way.

But it also contains an extraordinarily quirky little sign.

Having established that handwriting can be very symbolic and that 'tools of the trade' are often seen in a piece of text, or a signature (a pen or quill sign in the hand of a writer; that 'shotgun' in the hand of the sporty George I, reproduced in chapter five); let us focus on the capital T in the word 'Tuesday's'.

Does it call for too much imagination to see it as the coal basket in which the writer was hoisted so long ago?

And, is it not significant that the sign appears only on the T . . . the initial letter of the ship for which he was looking.

That is the most revealing mental 'banana slip' I have encountered for some time.

Memories of the night of Titanic's sinking obviously made a very deep impression on this man's mind; so deep that they were still manifesting themselves fifty eight years after the event.

HANDS OFF THE TITANIC

CHAPTER TWELVE:

Investigators

Chapter Twelve: Investigators

Captain J.M. Bridgewater, Sir John Latta and a solicitor by the name of Foweraker were three men who believed absolutely in Captain Lord's integrity. One might have expected their opinions to carry some weight. But they were not sufficiently highly placed — any of them — to battle with those who decided, in their so-called wisdom, to crucify an innocent man.

It was not the first time such crucifixion had taken place and it will hardly be the last. But this is no place for such philosophising.

Captain Bridgewater, marine superintendent of the West India and Pacific Steam Navigation Co., was the man who gave Stanley Lord his first appointment as an officer on a steamship (Lord had gained his first mate's certificate after serving his apprenticeship in sail). The date was December 1897; the place, Liverpool. Stanley Lord had just turned twenty.

Bridgewater, impressed by the young man's enthusiasm, appointed him to one of a fleet of fifteen ships of the Leyland Line, trading to ports in the West Indies, Caribbean Sea and the Mexican Gulf.

John Latta was chairman of the shipping company Lawther Latta. He did not appear on the scene until after the 'Californian incident' and Lord's subsequent resignation from the Leyland Line.

Sir John (he was created a baronet in 1920) offered Captain Lord an appointment with his London-based company, whose steamers traded primarily between Britain and America.

A.M. Foweraker was intrigued by the legal loopholes related to the inquiries into Titanic's sinking. He lived in Cornwall, several hundred miles away from the Captain's Cheshire home and the two never met, though they corresponded regularly.

Leslie Harrison explains the background to their association:

'He (Foweraker) had apparently been struck by some of the obvious discrepancies between evidence as given at the British and American inquiries and Lord Mersey's finding that only two ships, the Californian and the Titanic, had been involved. Although Foweraker's practical sea experience was limited to what he had acquired as an amateur yachtsman, he found the essential facts of the case to be so simple that he went on to make an extraordinarily detailed analysis.'

Foweraker contributed four illustrated articles to the Nautical Magazine and these were published under the heading 'A Miscarriage of Justice'.

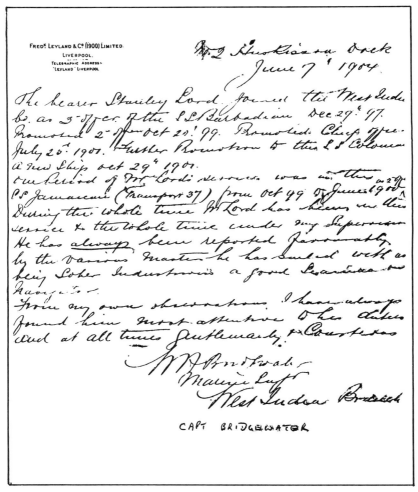

Fred. Leyland & Co (1900) Limited.
LIVERPOOL.
TELEGRAPHIC ADDRESS:
"LEYLAND" LIVERPOOL

N.2 Huskisson Dock
June 7' 1904.

The bearer Stanley Lord Joined the West India
Co. as 3rd Offer. of the S.S. Barbadian Dec. 29th 97.
Promoted 2nd Offer Oct 20' 99. Promoted Chief Offer.
July 25th 1901. Further Promotion to the S.S. Coloma
a new Ship oct 29th 1901.
One Period of Mr Lord's services was in the as 2nd Offr
P.S. Jamaican (Transport 37) from Oct 99 to June 1900.
During the whole time Mr Lord has been in this
service & the whole time under my Supervision
He has always been reported Favourably
by the various Masters he has sailed with as
being Sober Industrious a good Seaman &
Navigator.
From my own observations I have always
found him most attentive to his duties
and at all times Gentlemanly & Courteous

W. A. Bridgewater
Marine Supr
West Indian Bridgewater

CAPT BRIDGEWATER

Figure 63

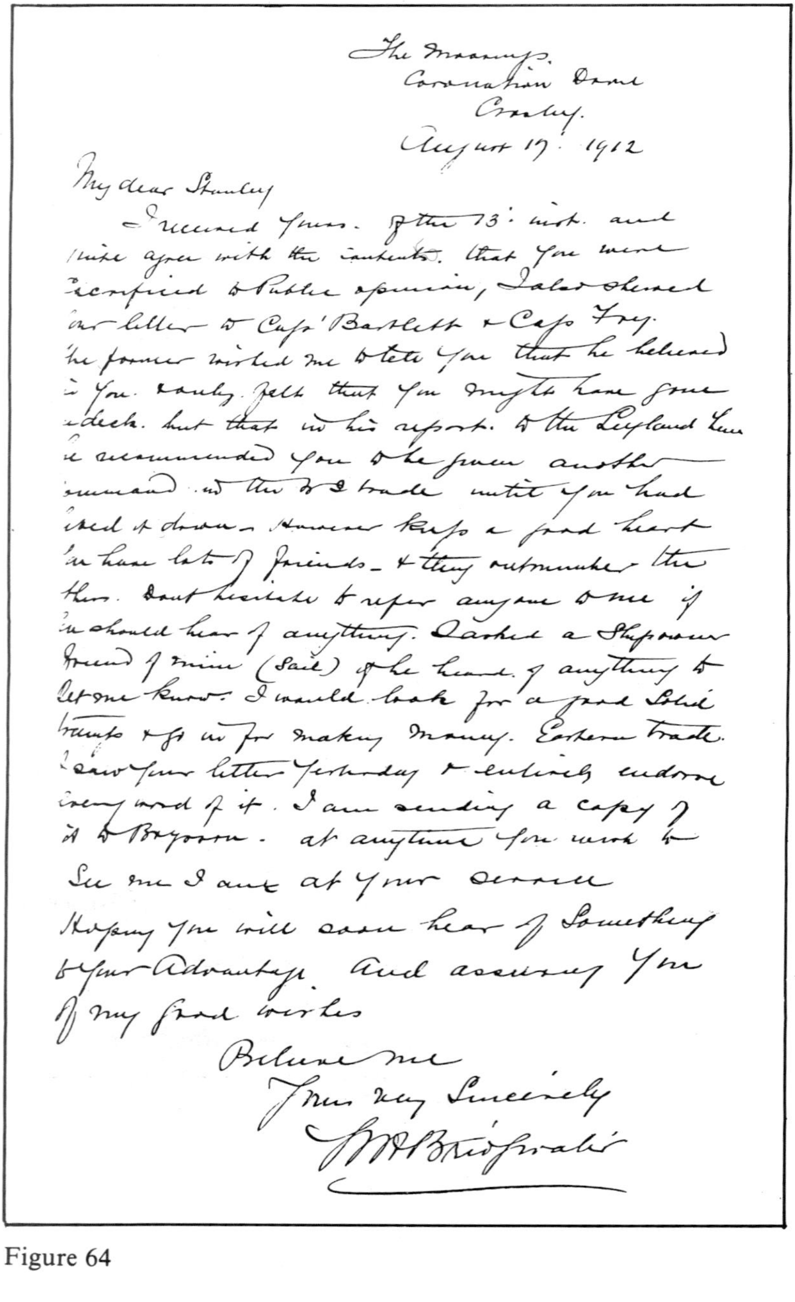

The Moorings,
Coronation Road
Crosby.
August 17. 1912

My dear Stanley

I received yours of the 13th inst. and quite agree with the contents. that you were sacrificed to Public opinion, I also showed our letter to Capt Bartlett & Capt Fry. he former wished me to tell you that he believed in you. really felt that you might have gone on deck. but that in his report. to the Leyland Line he recommended you to be given another command in the S.A. trade until you had tried it down. However keep a good heart you have lots of friends — & they outnumber the thers. dont hesitate to refer anyone to me if you should hear of anything. I asked a Shipowner friend of mine (Sail) if he heard of anything to let me know. I would look for a good Solid concern & go in for making money. Eastern trade. I saw your letter yesterday & entirely endorse every word of it. I am sending a copy of it to Bryson. at anytime you wish to see me I am at your service Hoping you will soon hear of Something to your Advantage. And assuring you of my good wishes

Believe me
Yours very Sincerely
M B Bridgwater

Figure 64

He presented his case, criticised Lord Mersey's finding in relation to the Californian and did everything humanly possible to right the grave injustice done to Captain Lord. A selection of handwriting samples from these three men are reproduced here.

Right from the beginning, Captain Bridgewater spoke very highly of his young officer and continued to do so, even after the events of April 1912, in which, he regularly insisted, Lord was 'sacrificed to public opinion.' Bridgewater lived in the Liverpool suburb of Crosby, just across the Mersey from Lord's home. Over the years, they saw each other regularly and became firm friends.

The samples reproduced here are dated 1904 and 1912 respectively . . . in other words, one before and one after the disaster. The first, a reference, was sent from Number Two, Huskisson Dock, Liverpool and reads:

'The bearer, Stanley Lord, joined the West Indies Co., as third officer of the s.s. Barbadian Dec. 29, '97. Promoted 2nd officer, Oct. 20, '99. Promoted Chief officer, July 25, 1901.'

'One period of Mr. Lord's service was in the s.s. Jamaican (Transport 37) from Oct. '99 to June 1900, as 2nd officer.'

'During the whole time, Mr. Lord has been in this service and the whole time under my supervision, he has always been reported favourably by the various masters he has sailed with as being sober, industrious, a good seaman and navigator.'

'From my own observations, I have always found him most attentive to his duties and at all times gentlemanly and courteous.'

The high form level of this writing points to high intellectual prowess. It is most certainly not the hand of a man likely to be taken in by falsehoods, or to describe one of his captains as being 'sober, industrious and a good seaman' had he been a drunken slob, as had been maliciously suggested by those of questionable integrity. Its balance, consistency and manifest shrewdness prove he was not the sort of person who would be likely to misjudge others. To do so to the extent suggested would be totally out of character for this man. There is nothing in his writing to suggest such a change in behaviour patterns.

It is full of warmth and sincerity; Captain Bridgewater was the sort of person who wrote and spoke from the heart. There is much fluidity of thought in this writing.

Even to the untrained eye, it is full of grace and eloquence. If I might digress briefly. A comment I made in chapter five about people's trades and professions, their 'tools of the trade' showing up in their writing. Notice the lovely flow of this hand: 'flow' being the operative word. Can you see how those beautifully curved lines and swishing movements conjure up images of the sea and its waves?

Telegrams Grenville, Bude
Telephone No 15 Bude
H. Link Manager

Grenville Hotel.
Bude.
N. Cornwall.

18 Aug 1913

Dear Capt. Lord,

As I am not likely to go up to London this week, I am sending you this line to remind you that on your present Insurance Policy we now have the Particular Average not uninsured while when you go on your next Policy we run the whole of it uninsured so that you will take the greatest possible care to keep clear of accidents and have this in view if unfortunately you were to get into trouble keeping expenses to a minimum. The "Anglo Mexican" now discharging at the same port as that to which you are bound is saving 13 days on the time allowed by charter but receivers are exacting £15 per day for it which is a [illegible]

move on their part, but formerly they often kept boats all their days; give on your arrival how long you are likely to be there and if they suggest dispatch money cable, but point out it sh. be less than £15 as Sandy is much smaller than Mexican, but you will see how the port jumps. When on the coast last voy: did anybody say anything to you about Titanic, surely they not. Kenricks have had the presumption to say they are surprised [illegible] the circumstances we gave you command, that you sh. have again gone to sea and that your ship is likely to suffer. I made short work of them and as I did not even mention the matter to you in London it serves to show it has not weighed with me and only mention the matter in case something was said and so that you may know I look at the matter the other way about. When the truth is known the chief will be brighter. Therefore you will have a good voy. Yours Faithfully,

[illegible]

Figure 65

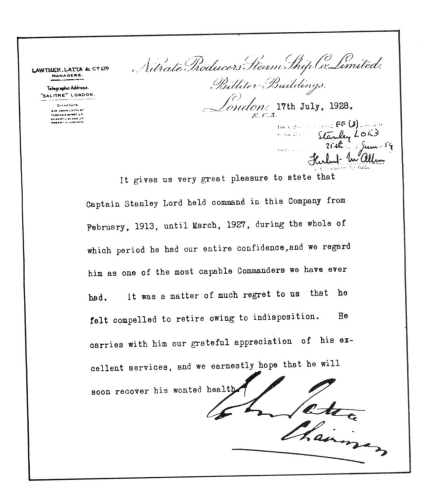

Figure 66

Remarkable, is it not, how one's duties (and pleasures — as with King George) can manifest themselves in this way?

More seriously, compare Captain Bridgewater's high quality and essentially genuine style of writing with those of Californian's more suspect officers in chapter eleven.

On the evidence of what you see here and on what you have learned of graphology so far, which of these men would be most likely to be telling the truth?

No comment from me this time. The verdict is yours.

Sir John Latta had a very high opinion of Stanley Lord and refused to accept the testimony of those whose minds were poisoned against him.

The earlier sample of Sir John's writing was penned in 1913, the second in 1928.

The writing is large, the letters long and sharp. Varying pressure points to an exploratory mind; that of a person who was ever willing to learn and to act upon what he had found. It could be decribed as a highly technical hand, showing the mind behind it to have been alert and creative.

Though in style and format, this writing is quite different from that of Captain Bridgewater; in its own way, it also manifests itself as that of a most perceptive individual: a straight thinker, straight talker with a sharp and incisive style. It is the hand of a man who believed in truth and justice . . . .

Turning to the 1913 sample first, we see that the writing is, in the main, quite spikey; its letters containing many sharp point. Added to its speed and rightward slant, the sum total equals quick comprehension; a penetrating mind. This is the sort of mind which could learn without exerting too much effort; assess a situation quickly and accurately.

The writing contains many heavy vertical strokes. In a generally positive hand, those strokes reveal an ability to face argument and controversy without losing his head. There is great strength of character here.

Like Captain Bridgewater, Sir John Latta, therefore, had a deep-rooted sense of right and wrong. His writing shows that he too, would be most unlikely to jump to the defence of a man who had committed a crime of negligence.

The long t bar reaching out protectively shows his concern for and loyalty towards his employees, but the jagged letter formations reveal that he could also be irascible. And good for him!

That is a very canny capital I. I have no doubt that those who criticised Captain Lord in this man's presence would have received the brunt of his caustic tongue. (In 1913 anyway . . . for he appears to have mellowed somewhat by 1928, when his writing, though still large, is not quite as spikey). . .

In his letter to Captain Lord, the downward pull of Sir John's writing shows how upset he was over the whole business of the Californian and the slur on the character of the man whom he held in such high esteem.

ADDENDA.

<u>Affidavit made by Capt Rostron of the Carpathia in N. York on June 4th</u>   Read out at English Enquiry by Mr Butler (for Mr Dunlop) - Official minutes p. 746.

25551. "I approached the position of the Titanic 41°.46'N., 50°.14'
on a course substantially N. 52°. W (true), reaching
the first boat shortly after 4.0. am. It was daylight
about 4.20. am. At 5. oclock it was light enough
to see all round the horizon. We then saw
2 steamships to the northwards, perhaps seven
or 8 miles distant,
Neither of them was the Californian.
One of them was a 4. masted steamer with one
funnel, and the other a 2 masted steamer with
one funnel. I never saw ⬛Mr Temple to identify
her.
The first time I saw the Californian was at about
8.0. oclock on the morning of the 15th of April.
She was then about 5 & 6 miles distant, bearing
W.S.W. true and steaming towards the Carpathia
The Carpathia was then in substantially the position
of the Titanic at the time of the disaster as
given to us by wireless.
I consider the position of the Titanic, as given
to us by her officers to be correct."
- You swore that? - Yes.
2552. (Attorn Gen) Does that state all the vessels that you saw?
I think it stated 2 steamers? -
<u>Rostron</u>. No; I saw one more, but it was during the
night previous to getting out of (up to?) "the Titanics
position. We saw mast head lights quite distinctly
of another steamer between us & the Titanic
?? .   .. .

Figure 67

'We regard him as one of the most capable commanders we have ever had' is the point HE emphasis in his reference.

Sir John, incidentally, lived to a ripe old age. He was just five months short of his eightieth birthday when he died in December, 1946.

Foweraker did all in his power to clear the captain's name and his attempts did receive some Press coverage, but not enough to challenge Lord Mersey's apparent infallibility.

One seldom encounters a hand as upright as this; or one with such a straight margin (showing the man to be, as the saying goes, 'straight as a die'). The character traits in this hand are all positive. Here was a most careful and fastidious man; the type never to be rushed into anything. On the contrary, Foweraker's style of writing show him to have been the sort of person who would spend hour after hour working on his project. He must have been an excellent solicitor, for he displays a marked ability to leave no stone unturned in pursuit of his goal. Hour after hour, he would have gone to great pains to find the facts. Every shred of evidence would have been pieced together, with painstaking care. Note how his words all fit together neatly, like bricks in a wall, as his case builds up.

Here then, was a real investigative thinker and one absolutely devoid of imagination (no grossly inflated upper loops; no distortions or 'banana slips' anywhere to be seen). He would never, ever, loose his cool. This is a most controlled hand, showing the writer to be the personification of calm, self-possession; someone who could look at matters without bias, accumulate extensive knowledge and only then, reach conclusions. Ever the perfectionist, he would give of himself absolutely to whatever he happened to be working on, be it a crossword, a client's case . . . or attempting to clear the name of the much maligned Captain Lord.

When Foweraker died in 1942, he bequeathed to the British Museum all the papers and documents relating to the British and American enquiries into the loss of the Titanic.

The British Museum rejected them as not being of national interest. Not being of national interest? Surely then as now, ANYTHING to do with Titanic could be categorised as being of INTERNATIONAL interest?

The deeds and documents were therefore offered to Captain Lord, who also rejected them (in his case, understandably, because space in his home was limited).

And so, they came into the custody of the MMSA, where Leslie Harrison, as general secretary, treated them with the respect they deserved.

He read them, catalogued them and passed them over to Merseyside County Council County Archives, where they are to be found today, on permanent loan and can be studied by advance arrangement with the Curator . . . .

No doubt, having been enlightened, impressed, moved and in some cases even amused, by what has been said about the subjects under analysis in the previous pages, newcomers to the world of graphology might still say something along the lines of 'Yes . . . well . . . that is all very entertaining . . . but surely there is an element of conjecture, and many of the comments must be tongue in cheek . . . .'

So, the next few pages are dedicated to the Doubting Thomases.

How accurate is graphology, they ask, pointing out that the character analyses conducted thus far have all related to people long dead and therefore unable to confirm or deny what has been said about them.

Point taken. Though memories of relatives and descendents are generally in accord with the findings, no one would dispute the fact that the memory can play tricks. The acid test comes when the subjects themselves are able to respond and say what they think of the observations. Therefore, the rest of this chapter concentrates on people who have done precisely that.

The six men studied hereunder are among today's leading 'Titanic buffs': experts who have devoted much of their time researching into the causes and effects of the sinking.

Having very kindly submitted themselves to my probings, they have — equally kindly — bounced back with their responses. I reproduce their comments, verbatim.

But first, let me introduce them to you.

They are, respectively, Edward S. Kamuda, John P. Eaton, Leslie Harrison, Richard Garrett, Peter Padfield and Michael McCaughan. Signatures and details are provided overleaf.

As has already been pointed out, only a limited number of character traits can be seen in the signature. The more extensive the sample of writing provided, the more extensive the character details to emerge from it. With more than one sample from the same source, other traits may come to light, either to corroborate those already found, or to outbalance them . . . thus to change the picture and facilitate a more a more thorough evaluation.

1. Ed Kamuda — The strong pressure of this signature reflects the enormous energy Kamuda puts into everything he does. The text of his writing (not reproduced) is less forceful. It is also virtually without slant. His public image relates almost exclusively to the Titanic Historical Society (of which he was a founder member in

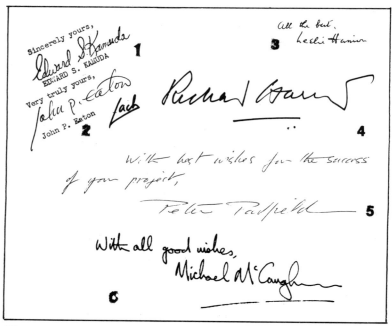

Figure 68

1 and 2. Edward S. Kamuda of Indian Orchard and John P. Eaton of New York; founder members of the Titanic Historical Society; secretary and historian, respectively. Eaton is also co-author (with Charles A. Haas) of much erudite material on the sinking;

3. Leslie Harrison, former general secretary of the Mercantile Marine Service Association and author of A Titanic Myth (The Californian Incident), William Kimber, 1987;

4. Richard Garrett, former staff writer of the Army magazine, Soldier, Editor of the Cammell Laird Magazine for its duration (1957-1965), author of innumerable books, including Atlantic Disaster, Buchan and Enright, 1986;

5. Peter Padfield, ex Merchant Navy officer, author of The Titanic and The Californian, Hodder and Stoughton, 1965; and

6. Michael McCaughan, maritime historian; author of Titanic, Ulster Folk and Transport Museum, 1982.

1963) and into that, he throws an abundance of energy. The signature is outward-going, but his text shows him to be a very private person underneath: warm hearted and with a keen sense of humour . . . he would appear to be rather less energetic in the pursuit of his private life and leisure activities, than those connected with the THS.

2.   John P. Eaton — (and alongside it, the less formal version of his name — Jack). This is a neat, lyrical and highly individualistic style. Its slight forward slant shows the writer to be a good mixer, but not so emotional that he is ruled by his feelings. There is a luxurious feel to this signature and, despite the large gap separating the 'p' from the other letters, it is all very fluent. The size of the 'J' compared to the 'e' indicates that he is known to more people by his first than his second name. The looping of the 't' stem intimates that he can be hurt and not show it. He is well versed at keeping his feelings to himself. The fact that the 't' rises above both capitals suggests some form of sublimation in childhood . . . that he was the sort of little boy whom parents (or siblings . . . or both) tried to undermine; but who carried on regardless, to prove them wrong.

Closed o's show an ability to keep secrets and the backward swing of the final letter reveals his absorbing interest in the past. The fact that it dominates the t is significant. Graphology, as has been proved time and again, is very symbolic. T, in this case, could be taken to stand for Titanic. Indeed, the same 't' dominates every other symbol.

The 'Jack' signature is a pastier, and therefore more emotional execution of the name.

3.   Leslie Harrison — This is essentially a cerebral hand. Its relatively small size shows excellent scientific — or at least, analytical — abilities; which point is reflected in i dots shaped like tiny little acute angles. The signature itself has both rhythm and balance. Printed capitals, which we have seen so often throughout the pages of this book, reflect the writer's ability to make himself understood. It is a strong and positive hand, showing many of the traits seen in that of Foweraker . . . i.e., persistence, thoroughness and great attention to detail.

The fact that the signature and text (again, this latter is not produced) are of the same size and style, show that the writer is the same in public as he is in private: the same to people's faces as behind their backs. This is a neat and tidy hand, from a neat and tidy mind: where everything is in its proper place. All compartmentalised, filed away and ready at any time, for instant recall.

4.   Richard Garrett — A heavy, sensuous and most artistic style, with garland letter connections showing a deep appreciation for and love of luxury.

The pressure is consistent and the writing very forward looking. Its upward swing denotes a kind and friendly nature, with final letters reminiscent of arms waving happily in what could be described as grandiose gestures. Versatility is manifest in the varying formations of the lower case letters, notably the 'r'. This writing is pure and rich; yet tastefully simple. Its unadorned letter strokes show the writer's inherent ability to stick to essentials. Religion figures prominently in this hand; only because of the somewhat unorthodox approach to it, and lurking feelings the writer had thought long gone. Graphology is very symbolic, as I keep discovering. The way we cross our t's is relevant. So is the structure of our G's. Here, the writer has stumbled slightly over each: almost as if there were some deep-rooted experience which had brought about his present attitude to his traditional upbringing, with its religious and other restrictions. Graphology, as the reader should know by now, is based on subconscious mechanisms and to the analyst who specialises in the psychological aspects, every little sign tells its tale.

Some slight underlying anxiety is indicated by the presence of dash-type 'i' dots and rather inhibited upper loop of the 'h'. But the tension is well under control and shows no signs of being destructive. This writer enjoys a good argument: particularly if it means being able to have the last word (underscore and dots)., but there is nothing vindictive in his nature.

5.   Peter Padfield — Here is a man of culture. A most aesthetic and pleasing hand. Its light touch points to refinement and gentility. Long, starting strokes suggest that the writer is in the habit of going to great pains in the preparation of everything he does. Some might call this writer a 'fusspot'; others, a stickler for detail. Printed capitals always indicate an articulate writer. Shrewdness is seen in the angular i dot. That long, exaggerated end stroke of the surname is reminiscent of G.B. Shaw and other great writers. Called a paraph, it denotes an interesting mixture of generosity and tenacity. On the whole, this writing is very forward moving, showing the writer to be a fast thinker: so fast, he could be described as a mental gymnast.

Connected writing equals logical thought sequences and good memory. Slight rightward slant shows he enjoys company but wide inter-word spacing suggests social discretion; possibly with its roots in loneliness. Nevertheless, absolute honesty is reflected here. Very nice. Very sound. You could trust this man with your life.

6.   Michael McCaughan — There is a very 'sporty' feel to this hand and yet, with upper and lower zones so much larger than the middle (showing the writing to be relatively small) it is also an intellectual hand.

. Oddly enough although as already stated, a graphologist cannot be specific about the sex of a writer; this has a very masculine 'feel' to it. It is what I would call — to use the vernacular — a 'macho' hand.

It bubbles with movement and speed and energy. Dash-type i dots which can sometimes be interpreted as indications of anxiety, here point to an astute nature. Low crossed 't' bars show excellent powers of concentration: one, which turns itself into a knot, points to a sense of achievement, although it also suggests that tolerance may not be this man's forte. There is just the teeniest hint of abrasiveness here.

144

The barriers can go up occasionally; he is not one for wearing his heart on his sleeve.

Nevertheless, this writer is discreet: a quality indicated in the way the last two letters of his name tail off.

Michael McCaughan's writing is quite fascinating. I would sum him up in three words: 'an intriguing enigma' . . . .

Do any of the six agree with what has been said about them? The ball is now in their court.

John P. Eaton: "Perhaps you might read an entire page of my handwriting before you draw a final conclusion; though actually, you were quite correct about certain aspects of my character." (An entire page? Chance would be a fine thing. Every single one of his letters is typed). He adds: "I continue to be amazed at your analyses of the Titanic-related people with whose backgrounds I am familiar. You have really hit the nail on the head with a couple of them and have come very close indeed to others."

Well, thank you kind sir!

Having read the entire text of this book while still in its embryonic stage and nurtured it — and me — through the post-natal period and the various stages of 'labour' before its final delivery to my publishers, Leslie Harrison justifiably feels much too close to the subject to be able to offer any unbiased comments. But he does admit that if my analysis accurately reflects any of his personal characteristics, he can only suggest that these must be largely the product of his professional training as a seaman and navigator.

Richard Garret and his wife both dispute the observation about his being sensuous and loving luxury, making the point that he is more at home in a country pub than a restaurant; walking in the woods with his dog than being in the city.

Now there are some who would call that sort of lifestyle the height of luxury and pleasure. Still, I take his point.

It merely emphasises the importance of seeing more than one limited sample of writing, because the signature on his second letter (reproduced hereunder) was indeed considerably lighter and less 'sensuous' than on the first.

Figure 69

Figure 70

As has already been pointed out by my shrewd friend, John P. (Jack) Eaton, a page of text would have revealed much, much more; only this correspondent is also in the habit of typing his letters!

Richard's response to my comments on the hidden trauma:

"The deep rooted experience has to be the last war: especially the years I spent as a POW. They affected me profoundly and gave me great cause for thought."

To remarks about religion, he responds:

"They are very true. I am a Christian without a church. This is something that is hard to get across. When I fill in a form for some reference book, I always write Christian under 'religion' and they inevitably change it to C. of E.

But thank you very much for your interest in me. I shall try to be more like your portrait."

Peter Padfield is happy too:

"This is most flattering; absolutely true in every detail of course . . . but haven't you omitted my bad points?"

Michael McCaughan does not disagree with the analysis either:

"I like what I read." he declares " . . . and my wife agrees that I am abrasive and intolerant!"

LAUNCH OF THE GIANT WHITE STAR LINER "TITANIC" 45,000 TONS, BELFAST, MAY 31st 1911
LARGEST VESSEL IN THE WORLD.

Figure 71

HANDS OFF THE TITANIC

EPILOGUE:

'The One That Got Away'

Epilogue: The One That Got Away

Francis Browne was a Jesuit seminarian, based in Dublin, where he was preparing for the priesthood. He had entered the Society of Jesus in 1897 and was renowned for his photographic abilities. His pictures of historic interest were regularly published in prestigious papers and magazines of the day.

As editor of The Belvederian, his college magazine, he was invited to go on Titanic's maiden voyage; but was, I understand, rather disappointed when his superiors would not allow him to take the entire trip. Nevertheless, they did agree to let him go on the first few days of that memorable journey.

So, full of enthusiasm and with camera clicking constantly, he travelled to Southampton, boarded Titanic, sailed to Cherbourg, then back to Queenstown.

His series of photos began when he boarded the Titanic Special train; then he took several pictures of the ship in dock, the start of her journey, the incident with the New York (where suction from the great liner almost caused the two vessels to collide). He snapped many of the passengers strolling on deck and produced a lovely portrait of Major Butt.

He also photographed a business card given to him. It reads: 'T.W.E. McCawley, physical educator, The Gymnasium, RMS Titanic, White Star Line'.

Another of his captions reads 'Titanic's first sunrise, taken near Land's End, at 6.45 a.m. on April 11'.

His photographs of the inside of the luxury liner in transit must be about the only ones extant.

When he disembarked, he was armed with several reels of film; one of them including a happy photograph of Captain Smith waving to him as the ribbon of water widened between the great liner and the tiny departing tender. As he sailed back to dry land, Francis Browne scribbled a few words into his notebook: 'She left Queenstown with 1316 passengers, 885 officers and crew'.

History does not record whether he expected to see any of them again. Fr. Browne was not to know that his would be the last photograph ever taken of the Captain, or indeed of many of his fellow passengers and crew.

When he learned the shattering news of what had happened to the ship, her crew and passengers, he wrote a poem in their honour; for the reproduction of which I am indebted to Fr. John Guiney, S.J.

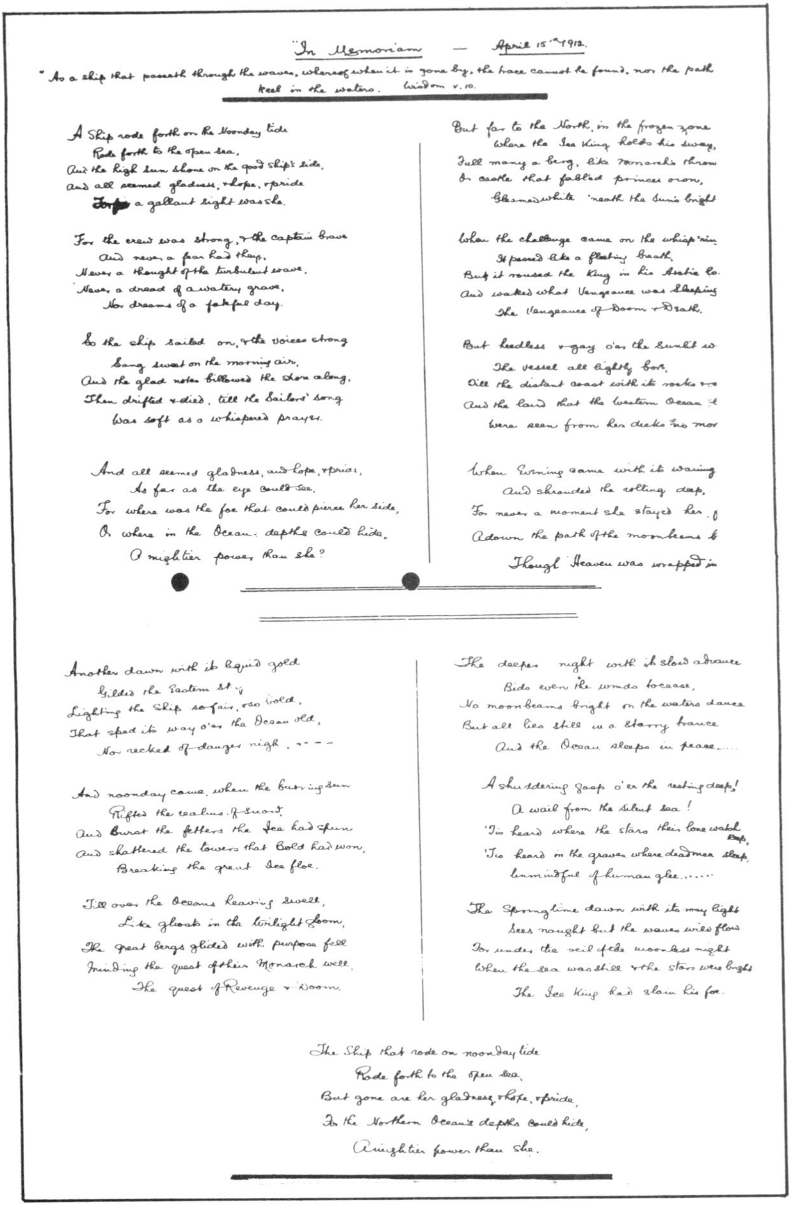

"In Memoriam" — April 15th 1912.

" As a ship that passeth through the waves, whereof when it is gone by, the trace cannot be found, nor the path
keel in the waters.   Wisdom v. 10.

A Ship rode forth on the Noonday tide
  Rode forth to the open sea,
And the high sun shone on the good ship's side,
And all seemed gladness, hope, & pride
  ~~For~~ a gallant sight was she.

For the crew was strong, & the captain brave
  And never a fear had they,
Never a thought of the turbulent wave,
Never a dread of a watery grave,
  Nor dreams of a fateful day.

So the ship sailed on, & the voices strong
  Sang sweet on the morning air,
And the glad notes billowed the shore along,
Then drifted & died, till the Sailors' song
  Was soft as a whispered prayer.

And all seemed gladness, and hope, & pride,
  As far as the eye could see,
For where was the foe that could pierce her side,
Or where in the Ocean depths could hide,
  A mightier power than she?

⚫   ⚫

But far to the North, in the frozen zone
  Where the Ice King holds his sway,
Full many a berg, like monarch's throne
Or castle that fabled princes own,
  Gleamed white 'neath the sun's bright ---

When the challenge came on the whispering ---
  It passed like a floating breath,
But it roused the King in his Arctic lo.
And woke what Vengeance was sleeping ---
  The Vengeance of Doom & Death.

But heedless & gay o'er the sunlit ---
  The vessel all lightly bore,
Till the distant coast with its rocks ---
And the land that the Western Ocean ---
  Were seen from her decks no mor ---

When Evening came with its waning ---
  And shrouded the rolling deep,
For never a moment she stayed her ---
Adown the path of the moonbeams ---
  Though Heaven was wrapped in ---

Another dawn with its liquid gold
  Gilded the Eastern sky,
Lighting the Ship so fair, so bold,
That sped its way o'er the Ocean old,
  Nor recked of danger nigh. - - - -

And noonday came, when the burning sun
  Rifted the realms of frost,
And burst the fetters the Ice had spun
And shattered the towers that Cold had won,
  Breaking the great Sea floe.

Till over the Ocean's heaving swell,
  Like ghosts in the twilight gloom,
The great bergs glided with purpose fell
Minding the quest of their Monarch well,
  The quest of Revenge & Doom.

The deeper night with its slow advance
  Bids even the winds be cease,
No moonbeams bright on the waters dance
But all lies still in a starry trance
  And the Ocean sleeps in peace.....

A shuddering gasp o'er the resting deep!
  A wail from the silent sea !
'Tis heard where the stars their long watch keep,
'Tis heard in the graves where dead men sleep,
  bemindful of human glee......

The Springtime dawn with its rosy light
  Sees nought but the waves wild flow
For under the veil of the moonless night
When the sea was still & the stars were bright
  The Ice King had slain his foe.

The Ship that rode on noonday tide
  Rode forth to the open sea,
But gone are her gladness & hope, & pride,
In the Northern Ocean's depths could hide,
  A mightier power than she.

Figure 72

The writing has a beautiful, lyrical flow. The writer was clearly clever and talented. It is an upstanding and assertive hand. But the most dominant factor to emerge is the writer's literary ability. This is indicated not only by the cultured look of the writing as a whole, but more specifically by its delta 'd's', epsilon 'e's' and 'g's' shaped like the figure eight. Inter-word and inter-linear spacing are excellent. There are no discrepancies in letter sizes; all of which factors show the writer to have been extremely well adjusted.

The baseline is straight and regular, indicating that, despite his undoubted aesthetic abilities, this young man kept his feet firmly on the ground.

There is an almost mystical quality to this hand. It is rather like that of William Stead (analysed in chapter nine). Both styles are remarkably modern for the period; suggesting that both writers were, in many respect, ahead of their time: richly endowed with the gift of foresight.

Different though the two men were — one being a Spiritualist, the other training for the Catholic priesthood, one being old the other young — the writings of William Stead and Francis Browne have much in common. Both were intellectuals, men of undoubted literary talents; of strong perceptive and intuitive powers: both outstanding and humane men.

Even now, years after Francis Browne wrote his deeply moving poem, he emerges from analysis as being a strong sensitive man. He appears to have had a mind capable of what would then have been referred to as 'thought transference'.

One cannot help wondering if he gravitated towards old Mr. Stead in the short time he was aboard the ill-fated ship, because from their writings, the two men do appear to have been strongly telepathic — both as 'transmitters' and 'receivers'. Such minds tend to beam out to each other however large or diverse the group in which they find themselves.

Did Francis Browne have some sort of inkling ('soft as a whispered prayer'?) of disaster, shortly before or actually at the time of sinking? Did his superiors? Is that why they refused to grant permission for him to go on the entire journey? History does not record their reasons. Nor does it record whether Francis Browne himself had any feelings of foreboding.

William Stead's unheeded warnings have already been noted. Did Francis Browne have a 'mightier power' to protect him?

Examining individual words and letters in his poem, I detect a few other pointers to his personality. His sharp, alert mind is evident in the way many of the words are joined together. The long t strokes, reaching out over many of the following letters, suggest a mind

Figure 73

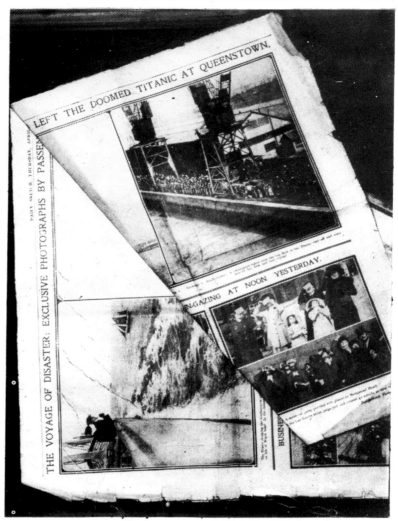

Figure 74

constantly on the go and it also hints at concern for others — which altruism is confirmed by the rightward swing of the lower zone of the 'y'. The capital 'S' shaped vaguely like a treble clef, points to a musical ear.

Here, then, was a man of integrity, an aesthete, an intellectual, who would appear to have been one of the most clever, but most down-to-earth and unassuming men on board the great liner. A man of compassion . . . and charisma.

Fr. Browne was ordained priest in July 1915, by his uncle Bishop Robert Browne, of Cloyne. During the years of the First World War, the young priest became military chaplain to the Irish Guards in France and Flanders: was frequently mentioned in despatches and awarded both the Military Cross and the Belgian Croix de Guerre.

From 1920 to 1922, he taught at Belvedere College; after which he became superior of St. Francis Xavier's College, in Gardner Street, Dublin. He died in 1960, at the age of eighty.

I can think of no more fitting end to this book, than to quote in its entirety, his poignant poem IN MEMORIAM. So, here it is:

A ship rode forth on the noonday tide;
     Rode forth to the open sea,
And the high sun shone on the good ship's side,
And all seemed gladness, and hope, and pride
     For a gallant sight was she.

For the crew was strong, and the captain brave
     And never a fear had they,
Never a thought of the turbulent wave,
Never a dread of a watery grave,
     Nor dreams of a fateful day.

So the ship sailed on, and the voices strong
     Sang sweet on the morning air,
And the glad notes billowed the shore along,
Then drifted and died, till the Sailors' song
     Was soft as a whispered prayer.

And all seemed gladness, and hope and pride,
     As far as the eye could see,
For where was the foe that could pierce her side,
Or where in the Ocean's depths could hide,
     A mightier power than she?

But far to the North, in the frozen zone,
     Where the Ice King holds his sway,
Full many a berg, like monarch's throne,
Or castle that fabled princes won,
     Gleamed white 'neath the sun's bright ray.

When the challenge came on the whisp'ring air
    It passed like a fleeting breath,
But it roused the King in his Arctic lair,
And waked what Vengeance was sleeping there,
    The Vengeance of Doom and Death

But heedless and gay o'er the sunlit wave,
    The vessel all lightly bore,
Till the distant coast with its rocks and caves,
And the land that the Western Ocean waves
    Were seen from her decks no more.

When evening came with its waning light
    And shrouded the rolling deep
For never a moment she stayed her flight
Adown the path of the moonbeams bright,
    Though heaven was wrapped in sleep.

Another dawn with its liquid gold
    Gilded the eastern sky,
Lighting the ship so fair and so bold,
That sped its way o'er the Ocean old,
    Nor recked of danger nigh . . . .

And noonday came, when the burning sun
    Rifted the realms of snow,
And burst the fetters the Ice had spun
And shattered the towers that Bold had won,
    Breaking the great Ice-flow.

Till over the ocean's heaving swell,
    Like ghosts in the twilight gloom,
The great bergs glided with purpose fell
Minding the quest of their Monarch well,
    The quest of Revenge and doom.

The deeper night with its slow advance
    Bids even the winds to cease,
No moonbeams bright on the waters dance
But all lies still in a starry trance
    And the Ocean sleeps in peace . . . .

A shuddering gasp o'er the resting deep!
    A wail from the silent sea!
'Tis heard where the stars their lone watch keep,
'Tis heard in the graves where dead men sleep,
    Unmindful of human glee . . . .

The Springtime dawn with its rosy light
  Sees nought but the waves wild flow
For under the veil of the moonless night
When the sea was still and the stars were bright
  The Ice King had slain his foe

The Ship that rode on noonday tide,
  Rode forth to the open sea,
But gone are her gladness, and hope, and pride,
For the Northern Ocean's depths could hide,
  A mightier power than she.

About the Author

Monica (Harding) O'Hara is a member of the Medical Journalists' Association and the Medical Writers' Group of the Society of Authors. Her other publications:

Understanding the Causes and Treatment of Kidney Failure.
  Wm. Heinemann Medical Books Ltd.,

Men of the Medical Laboratory.
  with Leo Gore, Mast Laboratories.

New Hope Through Hypnotherapy.
  Abacus.

What's New on the Health Scene.
  Pharmaton.

Scheduled for publication, 1989/90

How to Analyse Handwriting and How to Write Creatively
  Twin volumes, European Entrepreneurs Association Limited.

OTHER TITLES FROM

Countyvise